YORK NOTES

General Editors: Professor A.N
of Stirling) & Professor Suheil
University of Beirut)

John Buchan

THE THIRTY-NINE STEPS

Notes by Martin Gray

MA (OXFORD) MPHIL (LONDON)
Lecturer in English Studies, University of Stirling

LONGMAN
YORK PRESS

Extracts from *The Thirty-Nine Steps* by John Buchan are reprinted by kind permission of William Blackwood & Sons.

YORK PRESS
Immeuble Esseily, Place Riad Solh, Beirut.

LONGMAN GROUP LIMITED
London
Associated companies, branches and representatives throughout the world

First published 1980
ISBN 0 582 78244 9
Printed in Hong Kong by
Sheck Wah Tong Printing Press Ltd

Contents

Part 1

Introduction

The life of John Buchan

John Buchan is a fascinating and unusual figure in the history of modern literature. During his lifetime he wrote an enormous number of different kinds of books, about ninety-five in all, ranging from racy, widely popular thrillers, such as *The Thirty-Nine Steps*, to scholarly biographies and histories, and even a text book on taxation. His colossal literary output is impressive enough in itself, but even more astonishing is the fact that writing books was for him merely a hobby which he pursued in the sparse moments of spare time allowed to him during an active and varied public life as a journalist, lawyer, administrator, publisher, politician and statesman. His biography would make fascinating reading even if he had never achieved success and fame as a writer. That he should have combined so many different activities with consistent literary production of such high quality and such variety makes him unique amongst twentieth-century British writers.

John Buchan's origins were quite humble. His father was a minister in the Free Church of Scotland. John was the eldest boy, born in 1875 when his mother was only just eighteen. While he was still an infant the Buchan family moved from Perth to Pathhead, a small village on the Firth of Forth in Fife, not very far from Edinburgh. There he attended village schools and enjoyed an untrammelled country childhood. When he was thirteen the family moved once more, this time to the centre of industrial Glasgow, but every holiday was still spent in rural Scotland, at Broughton Green, a small village south of Edinburgh in the remote and mountainous Border country where Mrs Buchan's relations had for generations kept sheep farms. These summers spent in the hills gave Buchan a life-long passion for hill-walking and, above all, for fishing.

In Glasgow Buchan attended Hutchesons', a reputable local Grammar School. In 1892 he gained a scholarship to the University of Glasgow to study for a General MA (Master of Arts) degree. At the university he worked seriously at his studies for the first time in his life. He had come into contact with excellent teachers, in particular the famous Greek scholar Gilbert Murray, who had recently arrived from Oxford to be professor of Classics (at the age of twenty-six). Murray forged a close and enduring friendship with Buchan. At this time the General MA course at Scottish Universities consisted of seven compulsory but widely varied subjects: Greek, Latin, Mathematics, Logic, Rhetoric, Moral Philosophy and Natural Philosophy (Natural Science). After three years of this heterogeneous but stimulating programme Buchan sat successfully for a scholarship to Oxford, and in 1895 he left Glasgow to start a degree in Classics at Brasenose College, Oxford.

Before Buchan arrived at Oxford he had already begun his literary career. In his first year at Glasgow, while still only seventeen, he had persuaded a London publisher to let him edit and write a long introduction to a collection of the *Essays* of Francis Bacon (1561–1626). He had also written an article on fishing for the *Gentleman's Magazine* and completed his first novel, a romantic tale called *Sir Quixote of the Moors*. He arrived at Oxford, therefore, with a ready-made literary reputation, upon which he built steadily, supporting himself by journalism, writing for newspapers and magazines, by authorship and by reading and judging books for publishers. His most notable publications during this time include another novel, a collection of essays, a collection of short stories, and a history of his college. He also won the Newdigate prize for poetry and the Stanhope Historical Essay prize; he was made President of the Union (the Oxford debating society) and achieved a First Class Degree. In spite of this phenomenal success as a student (he even appeared in the 1898 *Who's Who* while still aged only twenty-three) Buchan did not devote himself exclusively to his studies. He and his friends were noted for prodigious feats of walking, rowing and riding, and he spent every summer back in his beloved Border countryside, helping on the farm, or exploring the mountains of Scotland on long walking tours.

On leaving the university Buchan pursued a dual career as a lawyer and as a journalist. In 1901 he had been called to the Bar, when he had passed the examinations necessary to become a barrister. At the same time he had become more or less editor of the *Spectator*, a vigorous weekly paper devoted to Conservative politics and the arts. Buchan lived in London, and he participated in the metropolitan social life of theatre-going, clubs and dinner parties. As well as his work on the *Spectator* he contributed articles to a wide variety of other magazines, and persevered with his novel writing. The list of Buchan's novels along with their dates of publication at the end of this book gives the best indication of his consistent literary output throughout his mature life. As a journalist he was famous for his ability to meet deadlines, to write with great speed, but with clarity and flair. Buchan never at any time in his life found any difficulty in the composition and expression of his ideas, be it for speeches, for journalism or for his novels. He seemed to be able to write in almost any circumstances: *The Thirty-Nine Steps* was written, merely as a pleasant intellectual diversion, while he was lying in bed in considerable pain from an ulcerated stomach.

In 1901 Buchan was suddenly plucked out of his London routine to start a completely new career. He was asked by Lord Alfred Milner, High Commissioner for South Africa, to be one of a small and highly select group of young men helping to reorganise and rebuild South Africa after the Boer War. Thus, at the age of twenty-six, Buchan found himself with huge responsibilities as an administrator.

Milner's young helpers, nicknamed 'the Kindergarten,' had been chosen for their intelligence, their intellectual independence, and their capacity for industry, and Buchan found this new life stimulating and exciting. To begin with his duties were to assist in the improvement of the concentration camps which had been established by the British to look after the Boer families who had been made homeless by the war. Though the intention behind these camps had been creditable (many of the Boer leaders' wives entered the camps voluntarily) the consequences had been appalling, with twenty thousand women and children dying from diseases caused by bad sanitation and malnutrition. Eventually doctors and nurses arrived from Britain and India and the epidemics were brought under control.

Buchan's second task was to organise the Land Settlement, redistributing farmland among the Boers and British settlers after the war, work which he found fascinating and hopeful, and for which he was well suited by his childhood and youth amongst the Border farmers and shepherds.

His experience in South Africa gave Buchan a life-long interest in African affairs and love for the African countryside, which found expression in several books and stories set in Africa, notably his adventure story for boys, *Prester John* (1910). But on his return in 1903 Buchan found himself ill at ease with his old way of life in London. Legal work and journalism seemed insipid and worthless pastimes in comparison with the testing and invigorating responsibilities which he had shouldered as one of Milner's administrators. And he missed the outdoor life, the long hours spent riding in the veld inspecting the farmlands which it was his duty to value and assess.

Nevertheless Buchan did return to the Bar and to his job on the *Spectator*. His legal work resulted in a text book on *The Law Relating to the Taxation of Foreign Income*, while his contributions to the *Spectator* gradually increased until in 1906 he became an Assistant Editor. Meanwhile his social life was burgeoning. As an eligible young bachelor he was much sought after at costly Edwardian balls and parties. In 1907 he married a rich, well-connected and intelligent young woman whom he had met at dinner parties and in weekend country house parties, Susan Grosvenor. A new period began in Buchan's life. At the same time he had accepted a new job offered to him by an old Oxford friend, Tommy Nelson, as chief literary adviser to Nelson's publishing company.

For seven years, up until the outbreak of the First World War in 1914, Buchan enjoyed the stability provided by his new career and married status. He worked hard with Nelson to revitalise the publishing business and together they set about producing a vast list of titles for a 'Sixpenny' and 'Sevenpenny' series of classics, which sold in millions and which were to be the forerunners of the modern paperback revolution in cheap book publishing. And naturally Buchan continued to write in his spare time. His journalism appeared in the *Spectator* and *The Times Literary Supplement*, while he wrote two books for children, a collection of short stories, and two historical biographies. Meanwhile also he was starting to think seriously of a career in politics, and became in 1911 Conservative and Unionist candidate for Peebles and Selkirk in his much loved Border country.

The Great War postponed Buchan's political ambitions just as it disturbed or destroyed the lives of so many of his friends. Ironically for such a man of action, Buchan was ill in bed at the outbreak of the war. Gastric ulcers dogged him for some time and indeed he was never to be completely free from the threat of illness and pain for the rest of his life. In 1913 he had been persuaded by the politician A. J. Balfour (soon to be Prime Minister) to write a 'shocker,' a popular novel like those of the writer E. Phillips Oppenheim (1866–1946) whose works they both enjoyed. The result was *The Power-House* (1915). In 1914 Buchan fought his irritation at finding himself on a sickbed rather than joining the army by writing a second 'shocker,' *The Thirty-Nine Steps*. He was at this time thirty-nine years old.

Nonetheless Buchan soon found work that he could do which would satisfy his desire to help the war effort. In 1915 Nelson's produced the first of a series, the *Nelson History of the War*; it was to appear in fortnightly parts, each about fifty-thousand words in length, written by Buchan. It was an immediate success. Gradually Buchan was drawn into a more official role as historian of the war. He was asked to visit the Western Front first as a war correspondent by *The Times*, and then on behalf of the War Office as a lieutenant in the Intelligence corps. Eventually in 1917 Buchan was appointed Director of a new Department of Information which was more or less in charge of propaganda and publicity about the war. There had never before existed a post like this, and Buchan had to forge the standards which he felt were appropriate: he insisted that the general public should not be treated like children, and consequently veracity and candour became the hall-marks of British internal and external propaganda rather than half-truths or deliberate lies. In this Buchan established a tradition which was revived in the Second World War.

Meanwhile the general public came to know Buchan as the writer of popular thrillers. *The Thirty-Nine Steps* sold twenty-five thousand copies in less than three months. Other Hannay stories followed: *Greenmantle* (1916) and *Mr Standfast* (1919); both were written purely as relaxations from the heavy burden of wartime work, though they reflect the contemporary events of the war. 'It is the most restful and delightful thing in the world to write that kind of stuff,' he wrote to his old friend Gilbert Murray.

At the war's end Buchan wound up his Ministry of Information with exemplary speed. He could look back on four years of varied and valuable experience. He had met vast numbers of people, from King George down to troops in the trenches. During the later stages of the war his close contact with the War Cabinet meant that his circle of acquaintances could now be said to include most of the important figures in Britain. He was now once again poised at the start of another career.

Yet the war experience had perhaps dampened his ambitions. Half his friends were dead. Politics seemed frivolous after the intensities of war, and he resigned as a Parliamentary candidate late in 1918. In fact for the next decade or so Buchan withdrew almost completely from public life. He bought a country house at Elsfield, not far from Oxford, and in 1919 he moved there with his family, now including four children. He had to travel up to London by train every day to work in Nelson's office and from 1923 onwards he was also a Deputy Chairman of Reuter's news agency, but his life was now substantially that of a country gentleman and writer. After the Border Hills of his childhood, the countryside around Oxford and the Cotswold hills were his second great love, and at least he had the time once more to enjoy being with his family at weekends, fishing, riding and walking. And naturally he never stopped writing: every summer from 1922 to 1936 there appeared a new Buchan book, adventure stories more or less in the mould of *The Thirty-Nine Steps*. Sales were enormous. *The Thirty-Nine Steps* alone has certainly sold well over a million copies since it first came out.

In 1927 Buchan was made a Conservative Member of Parliament representing the Scottish Universities, a seat which suited him well as there was no constituency work to tax his often delicate health. For the next eight years he mixed public life with the pleasures of his rural calm at Elsfield. He had many friends in Parliament, not least the Prime Minister Stanley Baldwin (1867–1947), so that his entry to politics appeared as a natural development rather than an upheaval. His first speech was a successful attack on government proposals to reform the House of Lords, establishing independence from a strict party line. He remained a back-bencher throughout his parliamentary career, but he participated fully in the many committees, and was particularly active in Scottish affairs, and in education and culture—for example he was instrumental in starting up the National Film Institute. As a politician, he supported a large number of widely different causes, from the protection of wild birds to freedom of speech at the BBC (British Broadcasting Corporation). Yet he still kept up with his work at Nelson's and Reuter's, and still wrote his novels, journalism, histories and biographies. Honours were piled on him. In 1933 he was appointed Lord High Commissioner to the General Assembly of the Church of Scotland, a duty which pleased and amused him as the son of a Free Church minister: the High Commissioner represents the British Crown at the annual gathering of Scottish churchmen and is the central figure in much colourful pomp and pageantry.

All the ceremonial of this post was good preparation for the last great change in Buchan's active and various life. In 1935 he was appointed Governor General of Canada. He was now Lord Tweedsmuir: George V had wanted his representative in Canada to be a peer, though the Canadians themselves would have preferred Buchan to stay a commoner.

Tweedsmuir fulfilled his duties with extraordinary vigour and thoroughness. As a Scot he had much in common with the Canadians, many of whom had Scots ancestory. His knowledge of farming, consolidated by his stay in South Africa, gave him a real interest in the problems of the large numbers of Canadians who lived on the land. And his love of mountains and of the wilderness meant he looked upon the arduous journeys that he undertook in order to know Canada better as relaxation. In spite of his age he travelled all around Canada, and everywhere he visited he charmed all he met with his informal courtesy, his friendliness and his unfailing curiosity into the lives and opinions of his fellow men.

On the political side of his job Tweedsmuir excited some controversy where he appeared to criticise the Canadian government for not having a defence policy (there were only a few years remaining before the outbreak of the Second World War). But in this affair as in all else he acquitted himself with good sense and dignity. He had to negotiate frequently with President Roosevelt of the USA and in his final years as Governor-General he was deeply involved in an attempt to unite America with the European democracies against the rising power of Hitler and Mussolini. At Tweedsmuir's prompting Roosevelt wrote to the British Prime Minister, Chamberlain, indicating his desire to mobilise anti-Fascist opinion by proposing a world summit conference, but Chamberlain, who wanted to negotiate personally with the dictators, and distrusted the Americans, turned the idea down without consulting his Cabinet or Foreign Secretary. In the opinion of many historians, including Sir Winston Churchill, Chamberlain turned down his last frail chance of averting the war in rejecting the fruits of Tweedsmuir's negotiations in America.

The outbreak of war was deeply depressing to Tweedsmuir, who had already witnessed the horrors of the Boer War and the Great War. His ceremonial duties were cut down and in 1940 he was due to finish his term as Governor-General, though he was sad at the prospect of leaving the country for which he had such affection and admiration. But he never returned to Britain alive: in early February 1940 he died of an unexpected cerebral thrombosis. Sixty-four years of constant activity, as writer, administrator, lawyer, publisher, politician and public figure came to a sudden end.

The Thirty-Nine Steps

The Thirty-Nine Steps was published first in *Blackwood's Magazine* in the summer of 1914 and appeared in book form in the following year. It has proved to be one of Buchan's most enduring and successful books, and has been reprinted many times and in many different editions and translations. Some indication of its popularity is the fact that no less than three films have been based (very loosely) on Buchan's story. The Hannay books have kept their appeal right through the past half-century into the age of television.

The Thirty-Nine Steps is not a literary masterpiece: Buchan intended it as an easy entertainment for himself and for his readers. But it is well constructed and well written and as such is worthy of study. It does not require elaborate critical explanation. Its meaning and its effects are not obscure or complicated. Part 3 of this book, the Commentary, examines some of Buchan's skills. It also includes a short account of the history and nature of spy stories, which follows on from the discussion of *The Thirty-Nine Steps* itself.

A note on the text

The British Museum Catalogue lists well over a dozen different editions of *The Thirty-Nine Steps* since its first publication by William Blackwood and Sons, London, 1914, until 1965, and each of these have been reprinted many times. No doubt further editions have now appeared or are in preparation. There is no standard or scholarly edition of Buchan's works.

A clearly printed and easily available modern edition is published by Pan Books, London and Sydney, 1947; 30th printing, 1976.

Part 2

Summaries

of THE THIRTY-NINE STEPS

A general summary

Richard Hannay, a retired Rhodesian mining engineer, is bored by living a life of inactivity in London. One evening an excited and frightened American bursts into his flat full of the amazing story that he is being pursued by a gang of anarchists who are planning to destroy world peace. The American, Scudder, has just faked his own death in order to evade his assassins. Hannay, half believing the story, allows the man to take refuge with him. During the next few days he hears more of the wild tale that lies behind Scudder's desire to hide. One evening Hannay returns home to find Scudder stabbed to death.

Thinking that he must continue Scudder's fight against the anarchist conspiracy in which he now believes, and realising that the unusual circumstances surrounding the death of Scudder may mean that he himself may be suspected of murder, Hannay decides to run away from London and hide in the wilds of Scotland.

The main part of *The Thirty-Nine Steps* is taken up by Hannay's flight and pursuit across Scotland, during which he only just resists capture on several occasions, and is helped by a variety of different people, including an innkeeper, a young aristocrat, and a roadmender. In spite of many lucky escapes Hannay has the misfortune to take refuge in a farmhouse which, it transpires, is the headquarters of his enemies, whom he has now discovered are German spies. He manages to blast his way out of the storeroom in which they have imprisoned him, and, ill and exhausted, takes refuge with the old roadmender he has met before.

When he is better, and just before the date that the Germans have chosen to set in motion their plot to destroy world peace, Hannay makes his way to a rendezvous with a high-ranking member of the civil service, Sir Walter Bullivant, who takes an interest in international espionage.

Events prove that Scudder's and Hannay's information is correct. In spite of Hannay's warning to the government, the German spies are successful in their attempt to steal secret details of the British and French defence plans. The only chance of capturing the spies before their return to Germany depends on the correct interpretation of certain notes (which give the book its title, *The Thirty-Nine Steps*) in Scudder's old notebook, which has been in Hannay's possession since Scudder's death.

Acting on a hunch about the meaning of the mysterious words, Hannay locates a particular house in a seaside town as the hiding-place of the spies. In spite of their brilliant disguise as ordinary English gentlemen Hannay eventually recognises them and they are successfully arrested after a fight.

Detailed summaries

Chapter 1: The Man who Died

Buchan begins the story with typical vigour. The narrator, Richard Hannay, depicts the boredom and dullness of his life in London, a life of idle ease, of 'restaurants and theatres and race meetings'. A few references to his past career in Rhodesia and South Africa establish Hannay as a man of action and decision. This impression is reinforced by the rough, colloquial style in which he sums up his situation: '"Richard Hannay," I kept telling myself, "you have got into the wrong ditch, my friend, and you had better climb out."'

Hannay is just in the process of deciding to leave England should nothing exciting happen to him, when a stranger accosts him. The man is clearly in a state of extreme anxiety and fear. He rushes into Hannay's flat, helps himself to a glass of whisky, breaking a glass in the process, and announces that he is in fact dead. Hannay believes him to be mad.

Bit by bit the intruder manages to explain himself and the situation which has caused his bizarre behaviour. He tells Hannay that he is an American journalist. While working in south-eastern Europe he has uncovered a vast international plot to start a war between Russia and Germany. He claims that on 15 June (we know from the book's opening sentence that it is now May) the Greek Premier, Karolides, will be murdered while on an official visit to London. The assassination will be contrived in such a way as to disrupt and destroy international relations. By coincidence, that very evening Hannay has been reading in the newspapers about Karolides.

The stranger introduces himself as Franklin P. Scudder, and explains that he is now hotly pursued by the anarchist conspirators. He goes on to describe an extraordinary escape from them, journeying across Europe in a variety of odd disguises. The anarchists, following him relentlessly, have now traced him to his hiding-place in London, a flat above Hannay's apartment. Scudder explains that he has just placed a corpse in his flat in such a way as to fake his own suicide, and he is now relying on Hannay, whom he has been watching, to help him hide from his enemies.

Hannay decides that he believes Scudder's story, strange as it is, and allows him to stay. Scudder disguises himself as an Anglo-Indian army officer, and Hannay's servant, Paddock, is completely taken in by this disguise.

The ruse of the fake suicide seems to have worked when the body is discovered the following morning and police assume that the occupant of the upstairs flat has killed himself. Scudder stays, but is still very nervous. One evening he tells Hannay more of the Karolides affair, but Hannay does not listen attentively, and remembers only a few details, a woman's name, the appearance of Scudder's enemies (one lisps, another has an odd way of covering his eyes with his eyelids so as to resemble a hawk) and something about a Black Stone. The following evening Hannay returns to his flat to find Scudder stabbed to death.

NOTES AND GLOSSARY:

the City: the business quarter of London, around the Bank of England, is called simply 'the City'

the old country: the narrator identifies himself as coming from a British colony by referring to Britain in this way

Buluwayo: a Rhodesian town

got my pile: earned a large sum of money

Arabian Nights: collections of Oriental folk-tales. Hannay suggests that England had acquired a splendour in his mind which was now proving imaginary

pot-house: a drinking-club or cheap public house

Armageddon: the name given in the Apocalypse (the Bible, Revelation 16:16) to the site of a great battle which will occur before the Day of Judgement: hence, any extremely destructive battle

It's a mighty liberty: the intruder tries to excuse the oddity and rudeness of his behaviour. All Scudder's speech is characterised by Americanisms

it suited the book: it was a desirable arrangement: a metaphor from gambling, the reference being to betting-books in which bets are entered

pogroms: Russian word for an organised massacre, especially those directed against the Jews in Russia in 1905 and later

Prince *von und zu*: German for 'from and to', referring to the typical aristocratic title which indicates place of origin and residence; loosely meaning 'Prince so-and-so'

Eton-and-Harrow English: the educated accent of well-known and expensive British private schools

he cuts no ice: he is unimportant and unconvincing: an American idiom

prognathous: with projecting jaws

Westphalian: Westphalia is a province of western Germany famous for its pig-meat products

played their last card ... they've gotten the ace up their sleeves: Scudder uses imagery from the world of gaming and gambling to describe the struggle with his enemies

***Mors janua vitae*:** *(Latin)* Death is the gateway to life

Epirotes: inhabitants of Epireus, the area of Western Greece near Albania

tip them the wink: inform them casually or secretly

Borgias: an Italian Renaissance family famous for intrigue and poisoning

an inn on the Achensee in Tyrol ...: Scudder's investigations take him from Austria to Hungary, back to Austria, then to East Germany, Paris, West Germany, Norway, and Scotland

no slouch in disguises: skilled at disguise

leeches: slang for a doctor

going straight with me: speaking to me honestly

pitched a milder yarn: told a less extraordinary story

Selakwi: district and town in Rhodesia

inspanned: South African term meaning to harness, here simply to hire or employ

gift of the gab: the gift of expressing oneself easily

Nawsty business 'ere this morning sir: the liftman speaks with the Cockney accent of London, elongating vowels (*nawsty* for nasty) and dropping the h sound at the beginning of words

churchyard face: a gloomy expression

in a brown study: absent-minded

clean grit all through, without a soft spot in him: this string of idioms expresses Hannay's admiration for Scudder's bravery and tough character

Blue-Grass Country: Kentucky, in the USA

other side of Jordan: death: the Jordan is the last obstacle before the Promised Land in Christian mythology

Stonewall Jackson: Thomas Jackson (1824–63), one of the Confederate generals in the American Civil War, called 'Stonewall' because of his bravery in the Battle of Bull Run (1861)

Chapter 2: The Milkman Sets out on his Travels

After overcoming his shock at the discovery of Scudder's corpse, Hannay searches the flat for clues to the mysterious murderer, who has already ransacked the place, presumably looking for the black notebook in which Scudder kept details of his discoveries. Hannay decides that he is himself now in a dangerous position: it is unlikely that the police will believe the strange events of the last few days, and the circumstances will certainly suggest that he is the murderer. He also feels morally bound to carry on Scudder's struggle against the anarchist plot. He therefore determines to disappear from London for twenty days, until early June, and then contact the British Government and tell all he knows. Meanwhile both Scudder's enemies and the British police will be searching for him. He plans to take a train to Galloway in Scotland, where he stands a good chance of evading his pursuers by hiding in remote countryside.

After a few hours' sleep he prepares himself for the escape, equipping himself with sturdy clothes and money, and altering his appearance by trimming his moustache. Just as he is leaving the flat he finds Scudder's notebook hidden in a tobacco-jar.

As he believes his enemies will be guarding the flat, Hannay makes his departure in disguise. He persuades a milkman to lend him an overall and hat, pretending that he is participating in some kind of joke, and then leaves the block of flats, whistling and imitating the walk and manner of the milkman. As soon as possible he discards the disguise, runs to the railway station and manages narrowly to catch a train for Scotland. The railway guard from whom he purchases his ticket moves him into a third-class compartment. Though accustomed to first-class travel and a life of ease in London clubs, Hannay now addresses his fellow travellers in a broad Scots accent, complaining about the behaviour of the railway official: his life of excitement, subterfuge and evasion has begun.

NOTES AND GLOSSARY:

Matabele War: a war between colonial settlers and the African Matabele tribe in 1893

I went over the flat with a small-tooth comb: I searched the flat very thoroughly

My number was up: I was in a dangerous situation and close to death

fishy: suspiciously unbelievable

make a clean breast of it: as honestly as possible

veldcraft: Hannay is skilled at looking after himself in open country (the 'veld') as a result of his experiences in South Africa

Damaraland: present day Namibia, or South West Africa

Bradshaw: a railway timetable

St Pancras: the main London station of the Midlands Railway (and for trains to Glasgow)

Wot's the gyme? What is the game? The milkman speaks with a cockney accent. Buchan prides himself on his ear for different accents. Compare Scudder's American idioms, and the language of the several Scottish characters in the book

Quid: slang for a pound sterling

Ere's the rig: here are the clothes

The impidence of that gyaird: the Scots lady is complaining at the rudeness of the guard, who has already doubted that her child ('this wean') is young enough to travel without a ticket. She asserts that her girl will not be four years old until August a year ('twalmonth') later

Chapter 3: The Adventure of the Literary Innkeeper

During the train journey Hannay examines Scudder's notebook, which is written in code. By evening, after changing trains, he arrives at a lonely and remote station in Galloway. He sets off into the moorland in good spirits, staying that night at a cow-herd's cottage. The next morning, still enjoying the pleasant spring weather, he returns to the railway, but to a different station. He intends travelling back some way along the line in order to confuse anyone who might be following him. In the railway carriage he finds a newspaper with an account of the discovery of Scudder's body and the arrest of the milkman in suspicious circumstances. As he passes the station where he had left the train the day before, he sees the stationmaster being questioned, presumably by the police.

Hannay decides to jump off the train while it has stopped briefly in open country. Unfortunately a drunken shepherd, thinking that his fellow passenger has committed suicide, raises the alarm and spoils the secrecy of Hannay's departure. Nevertheless Hannay makes his way to open moorland, choosing to rest on a hill from which he can keep watch for signs of a pursuit. To his horror an aeroplane flies overhead, obviously searching the countryside for him: Scudder's enemies are already on his trail.

After staying on the high moors all day, Hannay walks down to the lower ground and find a solitary inn. Here he partially confides in the innkeeper, a young man with literary aspirations and a taste for adventure. Hannay invents a wild tale of escape from Rhodesia mixed with partial truths about Scudder's murder. The innkeeper, convinced and excited by the story, undertakes to help him.

While staying at the inn Hannay works at decoding Scudder's notebook. Meanwhile two men, not police, make enquiries at the inn about a man of Hannay's description. The innkeeper throws them off the trail by claiming that such a man has already left the inn: he gives them a fragment of paper, supposed to be a torn-up letter, prepared by Hannay with the intention of giving them the impression that he is carrying on Scudder's work. The next day the men return, hiding their car some way from the inn. They are accosted by the police, who have been told of their suspicious behaviour by the innkeeper as a way of confusing the situation and diverting the search from Hannay. But, rather than wait for the outcome of this subterfuge, Hannay impulsively decides to steal his enemies' car.

NOTES AND GLOSSARY:

the Derby: famous annual horse-race held at Epsom in Surrey

my slouch: my cloth cap

blue-ribbon stalwart: member of a temperance society who has sworn not to drink alcohol. The joke is that the man thinks of himself as a teetotaller because he has given up whisky, the traditional Scots liquor, but he does not realise that brandy is just as strong. Buchan reproduces the man's Scottish accent and idiom

Martinmas: 11 November

sinsyne: since then

sair temptit: strongly tempted

Hogmanay: traditional Scottish festivity to celebrate the New Year

heid: head

hetter: hotter

twae een: two eyes

nip-nipping: taking continual short drinks or nips

weel: well

fortnicht: fortnight

bent: coarse, reed-like grass

'As when a Gryphon ...': the young man is slightly misquoting a famous passage describing a difficult journey by Satan in *Paradise Lost* (II, 943–5), the epic poem by John Milton (1608–74)

Kipling and Conrad: contemporary writers, both of whom wrote adventure spy stories prior to *The Thirty-Nine Steps*: *Kim* (1901) by Rudyard Kipling (1865–1936) and *The Secret Agent* (1907) by Joseph Conrad (1857–1924)

The nine-fifteen: the train taking businessmen to work would usually symbolise lack of adventure

I.D.B.: Illicit Diamond Broking, the illegal trading of diamonds in South Africa

Rider Haggard and Conan Doyle: Henry Rider Haggard (1856–1925) and Sir Arthur Conan Doyle (1859–1930) were writers of vivid adventure stories with fewer literary pretensions than those of Kipling and Conrad

nulls and stops: those parts of the code which are redundant and only there to help conceal the real message

Aquascutum: a raincoat of distinctive style supplied by this famous London shop

pump me: urge me to give more exciting details

Chapter 4: The Adventure of the Radical Candidate

As Hannay drives his stolen car along the Scottish lanes, he considers with care the new information which he has gained from decoding the black notebook. Scudder's tale of Karolides had only been true in a few details: the truth is more frightening. The book reveals a German plot to force Britain into a war while still desperately unprepared. Karolides' murder will be used as a pretext for Germany to act at first as a peacemaker between nations, and then to declare war at short notice and at any time. On 15 June a group of spies called the 'Black Stone' are planning to steal top secret plans of the disposition of the British navy. The theft is to take place while the plans are being exchanged between the British and French. Such information would allow the Germans to destroy the entire British navy with ease in the event of war. The words 'thirty-nine steps' are repeated in the notebook in a way which Hannay does not understand.

Hannay turns over this frightening information in his mind until his immediate circumstances force him into action. His pursuers, presumably having come to some arrangement with the police back at the inn, have alerted other police in the surrounding villages by telegram. There is an attempt made to stop Hannay, but he resists it by force. He now realises that the big car is conspicuous and easily traced, and regrets having stolen it at all. This anxiety is justified when the aeroplane which had been searching for him a few days previously starts to follow him again. He drives the car as fast as possible away from the exposed moorland roads towards the wooded valleys where he can more easily find cover in which to hide. As he rushes towards the bottom of a hill another car swings out of a private drive into his path and to avoid a head-on collision Hannay has to drive through a hedge. As the car plunges down a cliff into the bed of a stream he is by extreme good luck snatched from the driver's seat by the branches of a tree.

The driver of the other car helps Hannay up and invites him into his house. He is a young politician. Hannay now pretends to be an Australian called Twisdon. In this guise he can help the young man by delivering a speech about Australian politics at a Liberal party rally in a nearby town. Hannay agrees to this, and they duly drive to the political gathering, where the young man delivers a poor speech, full of foolish ideas about foreign policy. Hannay recognises its stupidity because of the information in Scudder's notebook. He himself tells the meeting all he can remember about Australia, ignoring the particular political emphasis required for the occasion, but his speech is successful. That evening, back at Sir Harry's house, Hannay tells him the whole truth of the London murder and its background. Sir Harry agrees to write on Hannay's behalf to his godfather, Sir Walter Bullivant, an influential civil servant in the Foreign Office, with whom a rendezvous is arranged near 15 June, the date when the international conspiracy is due to begin. Sir Harry lends Hannay a fresh suit of clothes and a bicycle and explains the geography of the locality to help him escape successfully.

NOTES AND GLOSSARY:

Dago: contemptuous expression for Mediterranean people, here meaning the Greek Karolides

billy-o: nonsense

pour oil on the waters: to pour oil on troubled water is a proverbial expression meaning to pacify

haugh: flat land by the side of a river

my left: Hannay's left fist

blessing his soul: 'bless my soul' is an old-fashioned and mild expression of surprise

comb my hair: figurative expression meaning to beat about the head, here suggesting anger

billed: among other things, a bill is a poster

ground-baited: a fishing metaphor. Ground bait is thrown into a stream to attract fish. Here the speaker means he has advertised his meeting well in advance so as to attract attention and interest

Henry Irving: Sir Henry Irving (1838–1905), a famous actor

knock her into a cocked hat: idiomatic expression meaning to defeat utterly

Mashona: a Rhodesian tribe

***bona fides*:** *(Latin)* good faith, honesty

'Annie Laurie': a well-known folk song

heather mixture: a thick tweed, of interwoven yarns of mixed colours

Chapter 5: The Adventure of the Spectacled Roadman

Once again Hannay tries to hide himself in high open moorland and once again he finds his enemies are using an aeroplane to hunt for him in the hills. He is spotted by the plane's passenger, and realises that he is now trapped. Proof of his predicament comes when he can see in the far distance signs of a systematic search gradually moving towards him.

Just as Hannay realises fully the impossibility of his situation, for there is no cover anywhere where he might hide, he meets a roadmender at work on the road. The roadman is suffering the after-effects of a drinking bout the night before in celebration of his daughter's wedding, and he is worried that he will be dismissed if he should be found drunk at work by the road surveyor, who is due to make his inspection that morning. Hannay, seeing an opportunity to evade his enemies, offers to take over the roadman's work for the day, thereby saving him from dismissal. They exchange some of their clothes, whereupon Hannay sets about disguising his appearance as thoroughly as possible, and then starts his duties as road-mender, successfully deceiving the surveyor when he arrives to inspect his work. Presently three other men come by, two of them being those who had sought Hannay at the inn. They are suspicious enough to watch the roadmender with great care while they interrogate him, but they too are deceived.

In the evening a third car slows down near Hannay. The driver, who has stopped in order to light a cigarette, is by a strange coincidence an acquaintance of Hannay's, a foppish and sycophantic social climber from London named Marmaduke Jopley. Hannay leaps into the car, grabs a driving-hat and coat, and drives off with the terrified Jopley, who believes him to be a murderer. Thus in yet another disguise Hannay drives out of the circle of enemies who were closing in on him. At a lonely moor some distance away, he restores Jopley to the driving-seat and allows him to escape. Alone once again, he reflects on the odd set of circumstances that have turned him into a vagabond, a liar and a car thief.

NOTES AND GLOSSARY:

bight: loop

roadman: roadmenders were employed to care for the un-asphalted surfaces of minor roads then normal all over Britain

wi' sair een, and a back like a suckle: with sore eyes and a back like a sickle. The roadman speaks with a broad Scots accent

heid: head

I canna dae't: I cannot do it

maun: must

nicht: night

dochter: daughter

waddit: wedded

fower: four
ither chiels: other people
Peety: pity
postcaird: postcard
yestreen: yesterday
fou: drunk
weel: well
I doot that'll no help me: I am sure that will not help me
they ken my kind o' no-weelness: they know my kind of illness; meaning they will see that he is drunk
motor-cawr: motor car
wad speir the inside oot o' a whelk: would spear the inside out of a whelk; meaning the Surveyor is painstakingly efficient in his job
you're the billy: you are a friend
eneuch: enough
bing o' stanes: heap of stones
needna chap ony mair this forenoon: you need not break anymore (stones) this morning
barry: barrow
metal: loose stones
frae: from
freens: friends
sicht: sight
fell: very
get-up: outfit
waur: worse
I wad rather hae yours, sitting a' day on your hinderlands on thae cushions: I would rather have yours, sitting all day with your backside on those cushions
muckle cawrs: large cars
oor richths: our rights
ye sud: you should
sax: six
toadying: flattering sycophantically
***savez*:** *(French)* do you understand?

Chapter 6: The Adventure of the Bald Archaeologist

Hannay sleeps on the hillside under the heather. He wakes to find himself once more surrounded by a cordon of searchers. For some time he enjoys trying to perplex and outwit them by running in unexpected directions, but he realises that the men looking for him have the advantage of knowing the locality well, and he soon takes to direct flight.

Presently he finds himself in the wooded grounds of an isolated moorland farmhouse. Watching him from inside as he runs across the lawns is an elderly gentleman. Hannay enters the house. The old man, who seems to be an archaeologist, immediately offers him sanctuary as he is clearly a fugitive. There is something discomforting about the manner and appearance of this gentleman, but Hannay is too tired and hungry to wonder at the oddly calm way in which he is helped to escape. As soon as the police have been distracted, Hannay is released from his hiding-place. To his amazement the elderly man addresses him by his proper name. He also hoods his eyes in a hawk-like manner, a trick which Hannay remembers described in the pages of Scudder's notebook. Hannay is shocked to realise that he has by chance walked into his arch-enemy's headquarters. Servants with guns surround him to prevent his escape.

On the spur of the moment he denies that he is Hannay, pretending to be a tramp called Ned Ainslie, who thinks he is being pursued by the police for stealing money from the car which Hannay had crashed into the river. The story is plausible enough to put his captor in doubt, and so Hannay is locked up under guard in a storeroom, while the fake archaeologist goes in search of his two henchmen to see if they can confirm that it is Hannay they have caught.

In the dark storeroom Hannay has nothing to do but explore his prison. He breaks into a cupboard in which is a torch and a large quantity of explosives. Judging that his captors will kill him as soon as they are sure of his identity, he decides to risk igniting some of the explosive in an attempt to blow his way out of his prison. There is a huge explosion, but he finds himself in the open air, though bruised and barely conscious. After hiding in an old mill, Hannay climbs painfully to the top of a tower-like dovecot where he cannot be seen from the house. He watches while his enemies search the mill and the surrounding area. It does not occur to them that he might be on the dovecot and so he stays there in safety for a whole day, racked by pain and thirst. At one point a plane flies down to a small secret aerodrome near the farm: fortunately it is too late in the evening to spot Hannay perched up on his rooftop hiding-place.

That night he climbs down, carefully but quickly makes his way out of the farm and its grounds, and runs as fast and as far away as he can.

NOTES AND GLOSSARY:

Mr Pickwick: the comic hero of *The Pickwick Papers* (1836–7) by Charles Dickens (1812–70)

jawing: talking uselessly. Once again Hannay adopts an accent and manner of speaking different from his own: Ned Ainslie speaks London slang

chivvied: worried
bobbies: policemen
on my uppers: running out of money. The idiom refers to shoes so old as to be worn away at the sole
grub: food
Lanchester: a now defunct British make of car
getting the pull on me: defeating me
Guy Fawkes: Guy Fawkes (1570–1606): in popular tradition a Roman Catholic conspirator whose plan to blow up the Houses of Parliament in 1605 has been remembered ever since with bonfires and fireworks every 5th November. Fawkes was tried and hanged in 1606
mill-lade: an artificial channel conveying water to a mill-wheel
vol-planing: a steep downward flight with engine shut off

Chapter 7: The Dry-Fly Fisherman

After escaping from the Germans' hideout Hannay decides to return to the roadmender's cottage to recover his clothes. In the morning he calls at a shepherd's house and buys food and drink, and a blanket. He then sleeps during the day and at nightfall makes his way with difficulty back across the moors.

Turnbull, the roadmender, does not at first recognise him, so ill does Hannay look: the injury to his shoulder sustained in the explosion is now compounded by a malarial fever brought on by nights spent in the damp open air. However, Turnbull looks after Hannay till he is better, which takes nearly a fortnight.

Healthy once more, and no longer pursued by either the police or his enemies, Hannay helps a friend of Turnbull's to drive cattle to the nearest town, which has a mainline station where he can catch a train for England. Eventually he arrives at the English village where Sir Harry has planned the rendezvous with the high-ranking civil servant Sir Walter Bullivant. Sir Walter is fishing. After the exchange of passwords, Hannay makes his way to Sir Walter's house where he is ushered in by a butler and provided with a luxurious bedroom and a complete set of new clothes.

After a good dinner Hannay settles down to discuss the events of the past few weeks with Sir Walter. He finds that he is no longer suspected by the police of having murdered Scudder: by devious means Scudder had communicated before his death with Sir Walter in such a way as to exculpate Hannay. Scudder was well known to Sir Walter as a secret agent, though he was not considered wholly reliable because of his preference for working alone. Sir Walter is astonished to hear that

German spies have found out about the secret exchange of defence plans between Britain and France, due to take place in two days' time. But he remains sceptical about the wide-ranging plot as detailed in Scudder's notebook, and is especially unconvinced by the likelihood of the assassination of Karolides. At that moment, however, he receives a telephone call informing him of Karolides's murder, thereby confirming the accuracy of Scudder's information.

NOTES AND GLOSSARY:

Samaritan: the parable of the Good Samaritan (the Bible, Luke 10:30–7) is a story of help and comfort given in spite of different nationalities, creeds and race

plaid: traditional Scottish tartan blanket which used to be worn as an outer garment

Burns: the late eighteenth-century ploughman poet (1759–96) so celebrated in Scotland as to be almost a symbol of Scottishness

whae are ye that comes stravaigin' here on the Sabbath mornin'? who are you that comes loitering here on a Sunday morning?

Losh: a mild oath

dune: down

Haud: hold

General Assembly: annual conference of the Church of Scotland

siller: silver, meaning the sovereigns

coont: count

cawr: car

speired: discovered

thocht: thought

syne: then

maun: must

gude-brither: brother-in-law

whiles: at that time

haun': hand

wersh-lookin' sowl: unpleasant-looking fellow

English tongue: English as opposed to the Scottish language

ae guid turn: one good turn

Border: the border between Scotland and England

lasher: weir

stickle: rapids

***alias*:** a false name. Hannay had previously called himself Twisdon

dog-cart: a light two-wheeled horse-cart

Great Scot: a mild oath

Marinamt: the German naval headquarters

Chapter 8: The Coming of the Black Stone

The following morning Sir Walter Bullivant tells Hannay that the French officials will come a day early in order to collect the British defence plans. Hannay, acting as Bullivant's chauffeur, drives him to London to prepare for the meeting between the British and French officials. He visits the police headquarters to clear his name of Scudder's murder, after which he is left to wander around London. Even an expensive meal does not quell his anxiety about the exchange of top secret information which is taking place, and while in a state of nervousness and irritability at not being able to help safeguard the vital meeting, he has the misfortune to be recognised by Jopley, the fop whose car he had commandeered briefly in Scotland. Jopley still thinks of Hannay as a wanted man, and attempts to apprehend him. There is a scuffle. Hannay is chased through the streets of London by a small mob of Jopley's friends and the police. He makes for Bullivant's house, where he is let in by the butler who hides him from his pursuers.

As Hannay waits in the hall the First Sea Lord, Lord Alloa, who is in charge of the British navy, enters the house to join the meeting in an inner room. According to Bullivant, Lord Alloa was thought to be too ill to attend the meeting. Presently he passes by again, and Hannay is astonished to see a flash of recognition in the face of a man who should have been a total stranger to him. Suspicious and ill at ease, Hannay phones the Sea Lord's home and discovers that he has in fact been ill in bed during the whole evening. Hannay bursts into the meeting-room to tell the shocked officials what he has just discovered: a Black Stone spy, disguised as Lord Alloa, has penetrated the top secret conference.

NOTES AND GLOSSARY:

play the deuce:	create a disturbance
Scotland Yard:	headquarters of the police in London
the Savoy:	famous London hotel and restaurant
Burgundy:	red wine from the Burgundy district of France
crool 'ard:	cruelly hard
graven image:	a biblical expression for a statue (Exodus 20:4)

Chapter 9: The Thirty-Nine Steps

The officials are initially unwilling to believe that they have been deceived. Bullivant telephones Lord Alloa's home to confirm Hannay's story, and the French Major-General, Royer, tells a hunting anecdote which supports the likelihood of the spy's deception. He points out also that the spy will be able to remember every detail of the British and French defences, and therefore he must be captured before the information can be passed on to the Germans. They have only a short time; as the spies are professionals they must hand over their information in person in order to receive payment, and therefore they must make their way out of the country as quickly as possible.

At this apparently hopeless point Hannay remembers the curious note in Scudder's notebook which he could not interpret: *Thirty-nine steps – I counted them – High tide, 10.17 pm.'* Perhaps this, with its mention of the time of a tide, is a clue to the spies' plans for their escape from Britain. Bit by bit he pieces together all the available information: the gang must choose a part of the British coast near to Germany; their point of departure must be near a cliff or steep hill with thirty-nine steps cut into it; the tide there will be at 10.17 pm in a day's time. An Inspector of Coastguards who knows the east coast well is called to help with the investigation. After several suggestions he mentions a place that seems to fit Hannay's description, a row of villas all with staircases down to a private beach near a seaside town called Bradgate. The tide times also match Scudder's note. The possibility that one of these villas has a staircase with thirty-nine steps seems to offer the only chance that the spies can be traced and prevented from leaving Britain. Hannay takes charge of further action, and sets off for Bradgate.

NOTES AND GLOSSARY:

salted dun breed: referring to horses, 'salted' means experienced. 'Dun' is a dull brown

Macaulay: Lord Macaulay (1800–59), famous British historian and poet

***mes amis*:** *(French)* my friends

Sherlock Holmes: the famous imaginary detective, hero of many stories by Sir Arthur Conan Doyle (1859–1930), celebrated for his ability to solve crimes by the processes of thought and deduction alone

Chapter 10: Various Parties Converging on the Sea

After driving swiftly through the night to the coast, as soon as possible the next day Hannay sends a plain-clothes policeman to count the various flights of steps in the cliffs near Bradgate. One flight has thirty-nine steps: the hunch seems to have been proved correct. Hannay orders the police to surround the house from which the steps lead, and also contacts the commander of a naval destroyer which happens to be moored out to sea in case it can help in the capture of the spies.

The villa apparently belongs to a respectable retired stockbroker. While keeping watch on the house Hannay sees the occupant walking along the cliff-tops, and looking out to sea, possibly waiting for the appearance of a boat. This behaviour fits in well with Hannay's theories, but he is still by no means sure that this apparently harmless old gentleman is in fact the sinister ringleader of the spies who chased and captured him in Scotland.

In the afternoon a large yacht moors out at sea not far from the steps. Once again Hannay's expectations are confirmed, for this is the kind of boat which he imagined the spies would use to make their getaway. He spends the afternoon fishing near the yacht and sees that at least one officer aboard looks German.

Later on, while spying once more on the house, Hannay discovers that there are in all three occupants: the old gentleman has two younger friends. They play tennis, and the apparent calm and utter Englishness of the scene and the naturalness of the conversation between the three begin to give Hannay serious doubts. He keeps reminding himself of his own attitude to disguise: when he had to pretend to be a roadmender, he lived the part as fully as possible.

That evening, filled with unease and foreboding, after checking his arrangements with the police, Hannay calls at the villa. He feels overcome by doubts about the true identity of the three men, and begins not to believe his former view that they are in fact spies. None the less he announces that he has come to arrest them for the murder of Scudder. They behave like respectable citizens of perfect rectitude, and are shocked and angry to be accused in such a sudden and absurd manner. Hannay, very perplexed, sticks to his story, but he cannot be sure that they are the wanted men because they behave with such perfect naturalness. Half mesmerised, Hannay agrees to play cards with them.

Suddenly he recognises a small mannerism: the old man drums his fingers just as he had done while interrogating Hannay in the moorland farm. Hannay now waits, perfectly certain of the accuracy of his deductions. As high tide passes his companions begin to get nervous. Hannay blows a whistle to alert the police surrounding the house. At the same instant the lights are switched off. One of the spies escapes through the window, and runs down the thirty-nine steps to the yacht, while inside there is a confused fight. The old man's last act before being apprehended is to blow up the stairs to prevent anyone from following his colleague, and he rejoices that one of his number has escaped. But he is swiftly disabused of this victory: the yacht has already been captured. Hannay's victory is complete.

NOTES AND GLOSSARY:

Union Jack: the national flag of Britain, so called because it is a composite design, containing St George's Cross (England), St Andrew's Cross (Scotland) and St Patrick's Cross (Ireland)

the Squadron: the Royal Yacht Squadron, an exclusive private yacht club: membership is signified by a flag called the White Ensign
Surbiton: a prosperous suburb south of London
chaffing: teasing
tub: bath. Hannay is reporting the kind of speech the stockbroker would use
I've got into a proper lather: the tennis has made me sweat excessively
handicap . . . a stroke a hole: he is challenging his companion to a game of golf
Browning: an automatic pistol
Peter Pienaar: this character appears in several of Buchan's novels about Richard Hannay, in particular *Mr Standfast*
pierrots: travelling singers, who have been entertaining seaside holiday crowds for money
rhebok: an African antelope
kopje: a small hill
black mamba: a venomous and aggressive tropical African snake
St Leger: an annual horse-race held at Doncaster in Yorkshire
the Fishmongers: a city guild, one of the ancient societies of merchants in London
a bit too thick: upper-class slang expressing dislike and disapproval
cut a rum figure: a slang expression meaning to look strange, out of place
***Schnell, Franz*:** (*German*) Quickly, Franz
***das Boot*:** (*German*) the boat
Der 'schwarze Stein' ist in der Siegeskrone': (*German*) The 'Black Stone' is in the victory crown

Part 3

Commentary

First-person narrative

Like many other novels *The Thirty-Nine Steps* is written in the first person singular; the story is told from one person's point of view as if that person were speaking personally to the reader. In this case the story-teller or narrator is Richard Hannay, a retired Rhodesian mining engineer of Scottish extraction aged about forty. The plot of the novel consists of the succession of unexpected adventures that befall him on his return to Britain. All these events and all the characters of the story are seen and described by him. Hannay is, of course, an imaginary person created by the novelist John Buchan as a mouthpiece for the story and ultimately for the view of the world which he wishes to depict. John Buchan and Hannay are not the same person, and when describing the events or style of the book this distinction must be kept well in mind. The author tells the story through the mask of the narrator.

In some works written in the first person the writer makes his narrator foolish, over-innocent or wrong-headed, and part of the pleasure of reading such books is trying to piece together what hints the author has provided to suggest a correct view of the events described. Perhaps the most famous example of this kind of book is *Gulliver's Travels* (1726) by Jonathan Swift (1667–1745). It would seem clear that *The Thirty-Nine Steps* is not ironical in this way, misleading or teasing its readers. Though Buchan is not Hannay, we are made to sympathise with Hannay throughout the book, and there is no evidence to suggest that we should view Hannay ironically. At the end of the story Hannay triumphs. His actions, judgements and view of events are shown to have been substantially correct, and his victory over the German spies reinforces and justifies values and judgements expressed during the book.

Style

The first-person narrative creates and colours the style of the book as a whole. It is an adventure story, a thriller, told by a man of action who is at the centre of the exciting episodes which he describes. Buchan makes Hannay tell the story in a conversational and colloquial manner. There are few long passages of semi-poetic description for its own sake, or meditations, or remembered flash-backs. When Hannay does pause for thought or to describe a person or landscape, the description is usually connected directly with the action of the story.

Hannay's address to the reader is colloquial to the point of being slang. This is especially true of the opening chapters, when Buchan wants to show the reader as quickly and firmly as possible what kind of person Hannay is and what kind of story he is telling.

The book's opening paragraph makes some of these points clearly:

> I returned from the City about three o'clock on that May afternoon pretty well disgusted with life. I had been three months in the Old Country, and was fed up with it. If anyone had told me a year ago that I would have been feeling like that I should have laughed at him; but there was the fact. The weather made me liverish, the talk of the ordinary Englishman made me sick, I couldn't get enough exercise, and the amusements of London seemed as flat as soda-water that has been standing in the sun. 'Richard Hannay,' I kept telling myself, 'you have got into the wrong ditch, my friend, and you had better climb out.'

Grammatically this is straightforward and simple. Most of the sentences are constructed as statements of fact about the narrator: 'I did', 'I felt', or 'I thought'. Buchan captures the way a person like Hannay would speak. Expressions like 'pretty well', 'fed up', 'made me sick' and 'got into the wrong ditch' all suggest ordinary speech rather than a more formal literary expression of ideas. This easily flowing conversational style does not make the book vague or slipshod in any way. The impersonation of the narrative style of a character other than the writer has featured in the best of literature from the earliest times. Obviously it has always been a major aspect of the dramatist's skill, but in narrative fiction too it is extremely common: the way Geoffrey Chaucer (*c.* 1343–1400) characterises his pilgrim story-tellers in *The Canterbury Tales* presents an obvious example in English Literature.

In spite of the apparent spontaneity of Hannay as a narrator, Buchan is in fact controlling the prose precisely and carefully. The narrative pushes on vigorously from episode to episode with economy and verve. Buchan's skill at keeping the story moving is masterly. He particularly excels at passages of swiftly moving action such as this, occurring near the start of Chapter 5:

> That made me do some savage thinking. My enemies had located me, and the next thing would be a cordon round me. I didn't know what force they could command, but I was certain it would be sufficient. The aeroplane had seen my bicycle, and would conclude that I would try to escape by the road. In that case there might be a chance on the moors to the right or left. I wheeled the machine a hundred yards from the highway, and plunged it into a moss-hole, where it sunk among

> pond-weed and water-buttercups. Then I climbed to a knoll which gave me a view of the two valleys. Nothing was stirring on the long white ribbon that threaded them.
>
> I have said there was not cover in the whole place to hide a rat. As the day advanced it was flooded with soft fresh light till it had the fragrant sunniness of the South African veld. At other times I would have liked the place, but now it seemed to suffocate me. The free moorlands were prison walls, and the keen hill air was the breath of a dungeon.
>
> I tossed a coin—heads right, tails left—and it fell heads, so I turned to the north. In a little I came to the brow of the ridge which was the containing wall of the pass. I saw the highroad for maybe ten miles, and far down it something was moving, and that I took to be a motor-car. Beyond the ridge I looked on a rolling green moor, which fell away into wooded glens.

Again the grammatical constructions are simple, immediate and direct. Each sentence curtly pushes the action forwards, without hesitation or unnecessary amplification of details. There are, indeed, plenty of good concrete details—the moss-hole into which Hannay throws the bicycle, the 'long white ribbon' of the road, the 'fragrant sunniness' of the landscape—but they are carefully chosen to fill out the bare bones of the description of the pursuit with a sense of realism. Every detail works hard to help to create an impression of authenticity. The nouns and adjectives are selected so as to particularise the scene that Hannay is remembering, but the most noticeable aspect of Buchan's writing in this kind of passage is caused by the verbs. Almost every sentence begins with its subject (often a pronoun) immediately followed by the main verb. The verbs coming as they do so often early in each sentence, create a sense of sudden decision and movement:

> In a little I came to the brow of the ridge which was the containing wall of the pass. I saw the highroad for maybe ten miles, and far down it something that was moving, and that I took to be a motor-car. Beyond the ridge I looked on a rolling green moor, which fell away into wooded glens.

Every detail is expressed through Hannay's actions: 'I came', 'I saw', 'I took', and 'I looked'. The sentences can be rewritten without these active verbs:

> In a little there was the brow of the ridge, which acted as the containing wall of the pass. The highroad could be seen for nearly ten miles, and far down it something was moving that seemed to be a motor-car. Beyond the ridge was a rolling green moor, which fell away into wooded glens.

But without the succession of active verbs the passage is inert. Its speed, movement and logical progression depend on the strength and simplicity of these verbs that express the sequence of Hannay's actions. Buchan even animates the landscape by his vivid use of verbs of motion to describe what is in fact a static scene: 'the *rolling* green moor, which *fell* away into wooded glens'. Very often the vigour and muscularity of Buchan's style can be explained by reference to this skilful and daring choice of verbs.

Description

The action of *The Thirty-Nine Steps* takes place against a series of carefully depicted landscapes. We are never ignorant of Hannay's surrounding, whether he is in London or the wilds of Scotland. The descriptions, especially of landscape, are exact and excellent in their clarity and freshness of detail. Here, for example, is the opening of Chapter 5:

> I sat down on the very crest of the pass and took stock of my position.
>
> Behind me was the road climbing through a long cleft in the hills, which was the upper glen of some notable river. In front was a flat space of maybe a mile, all pitted with bog-holes and rough with tussocks, and then beyond it the road fell steeply down another glen to a plain whose blue dimness melted into the distance. To left and right were round-shouldered green hills as smooth as pancakes, but to the south—that is, the left hand—there was a glimpse of high heathery mountains, which I remembered from the map as the big knot of hill which I had chosen for my sanctuary. I was on the central boss of a huge upland country, and could see everything moving for miles. In the meadows below the road half a mile back a cottage smoked, but it was the only sign of human life. Otherwise there was only the calling of plovers and the tinkling of little streams.

Hannay is made to describe what lies around him with the experienced eye of the hunter and mining engineer. Buchan himself was fascinated by geology and landscape, and many of his books contain passages of painstakingly accurate topography like this. Carefully chosen details create and enhance the effect of solidity, of an authentic, actually observed geographical scene. Hannay scans the countryside systematically on all four sides and pays tribute to its variety and complexity. There are mountains and plains, there is space and narrowness, there is colour, and, in the final sentence, noise. Once again a verb lends a special vividness to an account of an inanimate scene. The plain before him is a 'blue dimness' which '*melted* into the distance.' An object, the plain, is first made abstract and then given a liquidity and activity which surprises the reader by its freshness and accuracy. After this imaginative transformation of the plain come more prosaic figurative descriptions to particularise the hills on each side of Hannay. They are 'round-shouldered', again giving them human qualities, and 'as smooth as pancakes'. Their familiar, almost domestic appearance is contrasted with the 'high heathery mountains', and the muscular 'big knot of hill', on which Hannay has already sheltered: this is part of an implicit pattern of contrasts throughout the passage, which adds to its effect, and draws the whole description together, perhaps even hinting at the apparent security yet imminent peril of Hannay's situation.

Characterisation

In the descriptions of Hannay's surroundings Buchan amplifies the intrinsic realism of the colloquial first person narrative by selecting details and vivid figurative language in order to imbue the story with an impression of authenticity, of particular objects and events seen by a particular person at a particular time. The writer's aim is the same in the depiction of the minor characters that Hannay meets. They need to be described with a similar sense of particularity, even oddity, to make them interesting, memorable and even believable for the reader, for the special traits that Buchan gives to his minor characters serve to underline the special qualities of Hannay as adventurer, observer, and narrator.

Minor characters

Many of the chapter titles of *The Thirty-Nine Steps* make intriguing references to the book's minor characters. From Chapters 3 to 7 there is a sequence of titles based on the people that Hannay meets: 'The Adventure of the Literary Innkeeper' is followed by three more 'Adventures', those of 'The Radical Candidate', 'The Spectacled Roadman', and 'The Bald Archaeologist', and finally 'The Dry-Fly Fisherman'. Buchan has striven to introduce Hannay to a series of widely differing types and personalities, and each one is made as individual a creation as possible. In focusing so much attention on the people Hannay meets, Buchan might be emulating the famous Scottish novelist Sir Walter Scott (1771–1832), who was particularly well-known for his minor characters, and whose work Buchan admired greatly. Almost certainly Buchan would have had Scott in mind in the sections where the characters use dialect forms of English. The spectacled roadman, for example, Alexander Turnbull, speaks the Scots tongue with consistent vigour. Scott was among the first novelists to attempt the transcription of dialect speech. Buchan gives all his characters identifiable voices of their own, from the Americanisms of

Franklin P. Scudder right through to the jocularities of the three German spies in their guise as jolly English gentlemen. This ability to capture different forms and patterns of speech is something that Buchan seems to enjoy and at which he excels in his novels. It is perhaps surprising that he never used this talent in its more natural setting by writing for the stage.

Even the most minor characters are given traits that particularise them and make Hannay's observation of them seem authentic. The milkman, from whom Hannay borrows the disguise that he uses to escape from his apartment in Chapter 2, appears only very briefly in the book, yet his appearance and personality are suggested by a few broad but carefully selected details:

> At one minute after the quarter to seven I heard the rattle of the cans outside. I opened the front door, and there was my man, singling out my cans from a bunch he carried and whistling through his teeth. He jumped a bit at the sight of me.
>
> 'Come in here a moment,' I said. 'I want a word with you.' And led him into the dining-room.
>
> 'I reckon you're a bit of a sportsman,' I said, 'and I want you to do me a service. Lend me your cap and overall for ten minutes, and here's a sovereign for you.' His eyes opened at the sight of the gold, and he grinned broadly. 'Wot's the gyme?' he asked.
>
> 'A bet,' I said. 'I haven't time to explain, but to win it I've got to be a milkman for the next ten minutes. All you've got to do is to stay here till I come back. You'll be a bit late, but nobody will complain, and you'll have that quid for yourself.'
>
> 'Right-oh!' he said cheerily. 'I ain't the man to spoil a bit of sport. 'Ere's the rig, guv'nor.'
>
> I stuck on his flat blue hat and his white overall, picked up the cans, banged my door, and went whistling downstairs. The porter at the foot told me to shut my jaw, which sounded as if my make-up was adequate.

The most noticeable characteristic, of course, is his cockney accent. His cheeriness makes his acquiescence in Hannay's plan more credible; he grins broadly at Hannay's odd request, he is always whistling, and he walks with a jaunty swing. These last two traits are imitated by Hannay in his escape from the building. Hannay's first view of the milkman creates a vignette which clearly shows Buchan's talent for the selection of vivid detail. As Hannay opens the front door, the milkman is described in the act of selecting the appropriate milk-can, and whistling through his teeth. It is unnecessary from the point of view of the advancement of the plot that we should learn these irrelevant facts about the milkman, yet it is exactly this kind of redundant detail that gives Buchan's prose its vivacity and realism. Nor is the milkman whistling normally, but he is whistling *through his teeth*, providing yet another layer of detail.

The longer and more complete characterisations that occur throughout the book are built up in the same way by Buchan. A character's speech gives us the essential knowledge of his personality, and this initial understanding is backed up by a few selected visual details. Alexander Turnbull, the roadmender, helps Hannay out of a difficult situation in Chapter 5:

> Then in a tiny bight of road, beside a heap of stones, I found the roadman. He had just arrived, and was wearily flinging down his hammer. He looked at me with a fishy eye and yawned.
>
> 'Confoond the day I ever left the herdin'!' he said, as if to the world at large. 'There I was my ain maister. Now I'm a slave to the Government, tethered to the roadside, wi' sair een, and a back like a suckle.'
>
> He took up the hammer, struck a stone, dropped the implement with an oath, and put both hands to his ears. 'Mercy on me! My heid's burstin'!' he cried.
>
> He was a wild figure, about my own size but much bent, with a week's beard on his chin, and a pair of big horn spectacles.

Like the milkman, he is first seen participating in an action that helps define his job and character. Here he is flinging down his hammer, rather than picking it up, which leads forward to the explanation of his 'fishy eye' and general exhaustion. The way we are introduced to Turnbull is typical of Buchan's pleasure in ironic reversals: he likes to lead his reader up to some kind of climax, and then frustrate the expectations which he has set up by an apparent (but not actual) change of direction in the story. At this point Hannay is hemmed in on all sides by his enemies, and trying to find some way of hiding or escaping, but his resourcefulness is defeated by the barrenness of the countryside. The excitement of the chase is suddenly suspended, in an almost comical manner, by the monologue of a drunken roadmender, who is cursing his job because of a hangover. Hannay seems to enjoy the incongruity of the situation, and Buchan himself delights in strange encounters between his characters. The 'big horn spectacles' add another touch of oddity to the encounter. As if addressing the world in general, for he seems not at all surprised or even interested in Hannay's sudden appearance, Turnbull explains in his broad and compelling Scots language the cause of his hangover: he has spent the previous night celebrating the marriage of his only daughter. And he is particularly at risk this very morning because a new and officious road surveyor is about to check his handiwork, and if found drunk he will surely be dismissed. Buchan chooses to present Turnbull at a moment when his loquaciousness is natural. He surrounds him with a web of circumstance, a whole pattern of background facts, likely attitudes and feelings. We learn almost immediately of his job, his past, and his family life. Later when Hannay disguises himself as Turnbull, we know something more of his outward appearance, and, perhaps more fascinating, in Hannay's description of how he assumes Turnbull's role, Buchan presents the reader with an imaginative entry into the roadmender's personality and being:

> Then I set to work to dress for the part. I opened the collar of my shirt—it was a vulgar blue-and-white check such as ploughmen wear—and revealed a neck as brown as any tinker's. I rolled up my sleeves, and there was a forearm which might have been a blacksmith's, sunburnt and rough with old scars. I got my boots and trouser-legs all white from the dust of the road, and hitched up my trousers, tying them with string below the knee. Then I set to work on my face. With a handful of dust I made a watermark round my neck, the place where Mr Turnbull's Sunday ablutions might be expected to stop. I rubbed a good deal of dirt also into the sunburn of my cheeks. A roadman's eyes would no doubt be a little inflamed, so I connived to get some dust in both of mine, and by dint of vigorous rubbing produced a bleary effect.
>
> The sandwiches Sir Harry had given me had gone off with my coat, but the roadman's lunch, tied up in a red handkerchief, was at my disposal. I ate with great relish several of the thick slabs of scone and cheese and drank a little of the cold tea. In the handkerchief was a local paper tied with string and addressed to Mr Turnbull—obviously meant to solace his midday leisure. I did up the bundle again, and put the paper conspicuously beside it. My boots did not satisfy me, but by dint of kicking among the stones I reduced them to the granite-like surface which marks a roadman's footgear. Then I bit and scraped my fingernails till the edges were all cracked and uneven. The men I was matched against would miss no detail. I broke one of the bootlaces and retied it in a clumsy knot, and loosed the other so that my thick grey socks bulged over the uppers. Still no sign of anything on the road. The motor I had observed half an hour ago must have gone home.
>
> My toilet complete, I took up the barrow and began my journeys to and from the quarry a hundred yards off.

This attempt by Hannay to *be* the roadmender provides a peculiarly inward view of a minor character. The aspects of his own appearance and apparel which Hannay has to change in order to achieve his disguise make our perception of Turnbull unusually intimately realised and comprehensible: we are led to imagine his reality as a person from inside, as well as from his outside appearance and actions. Buchan returns frequently to this special interest in disguise, both in *The Thirty-Nine Steps* and his other adventure stories.

Turnbull appears later in the plot – he nurses Hannay through a bout of malaria and hides him from his enemies – and we see further aspects of his character, his kindness, honesty and pride. He is a minor and in many respects an insignificant figure so far as the plot as a whole is concerned. For example, he never knows anything of the political background to Hannay's plight. Yet Buchan enjoys creating as multi-dimensional and as detailed a characterisation as possible without digressing from the advancing action. All the characters whom Hannay meets, from Franklin P. Scudder to Sir Walter Bullivant, are created with equal concern for their truth to life and out of a delight in the variety of human nature. This wide-ranging characterisation testifies to the intelligence, liveliness, curiosity and powers of observation of John Buchan as an author, via his narrator Hannay. The book as a whole elaborates a coherent series of attitudes through Hannay's descriptions of events and people, and the most important characterisation is, of course, the created personality of the narrator.

Richard Hannay

Richard Hannay is a man of action, a swift thinker and a sharp observer of things and people. The plot of *The Thirty-Nine Steps*, consisting as it does of a journey, allows him to meet a wide range of different kinds of people, and it is through his attitude to this spectrum of different types and classes that we come to appreciate his view of life. He likes to find good in people. He is patient at the folly of youth, as his attitude to Sir Harry, 'The Radical Candidate', shows. He discards the 'poisonous rubbish' of his political views, and prefers to concentrate on his ordinary qualities:

> But if he was lukewarm politically, he had strong views on other things. He found out I knew a bit about horses, and jawed away about the Derby entries; and he was full of plans for improving his shooting. Altogether a very clear, decent, callow young man.

There is a pleasant irony for the reader in the way Hannay turns aside the young man's mistaken political views and approves his sporting instincts, implying that a man's knowledge of horse-racing is a truer gauge of quality than his ideological standpoint. As a judge of people, Hannay is shown to be unerringly correct by instinct. His judgement cuts across class barriers to find the best or worst in the people he meets. He likes and trusts ordinary people, especially the shepherds and country dwellers that he meets in Scotland, and his belief in their good qualities is repaid when the roadmender nurses him through his bout of malaria. Hannay is uncomfortable only with the middle-class person, the type whom the world would judge as reliable and successful:

> A man of my sort, who has travelled about the world in rough places, gets on perfectly well with two classes, what you may call the upper and the lower. He understands them and they understand him. I was at home with herds and tramps and roadmen, and I was sufficiently at my ease with people like Sir Walter and the men I had met the night before. I can't explain why, but it is a fact. But what fellows like me don't understand is the great comfortable, satisfied middle-class world, the folk that live in villas and suburbs. He doesn't know how they look at things, he doesn't understand their conventions and he is as shy of them as of a black mamba. (Chapter 10)

Though this is certainly a kind of snobbery, Hannay dislikes snobs, as shown in his contempt for Marmaduke Jopley, the 'offence to creation', whose car he steals at the end of Chapter 4 and whose teeth he breaks while in London awaiting the coming of the Black Stone in Chapter 8. In his distaste for middle-class respectability Hannay at least blames himself for his own lack of understanding. Most of Buchan's readers would be drawn from the 'middle-class world,' and Hannay's affected dislike for their world is a measure of the book's deliberate escapism.

Hannay dislikes evil, and has no qualms about identifying it in his enemies: the anarchist plans of the Black Stone are evil. Yet his views are characterised by a tough fairness which is in itself admirable. At the book's end he is prepared to admit that his arch-enemy was more than just a scoundrel: '...I realised for the first time the terrible thing that I had been up against. This man was more than a spy; in his foul way he had been a patriot.' But enemy patriotism can only emerge in a 'foul way.' Hannay's insight does not undercut his sense of triumph at victory over his enemies. The politics of the book are in the main a simple issue of good against evil, black against white.

The Thirty-Nine Steps is not a particularly violent book, but there are several occasions when Hannay lashes out with his fists at more or less innocent bystanders, not the least instance being his attack on Jopley. Admittedly this outburst is partially excused by the circumstances, the tenseness of waiting for events to unfold, but Hannay seems to derive some savage satisfaction from smashing Jopley's teeth, which is perhaps a lapse in the tough fairness with which Buchan has endowed his protagonist, though it is entirely consonant with the rest of Hannay's character as a man of action, preferring deeds to words, hating inactivity, and not being frightened of pitting himself against both anarchist murderers and the British police force. Hannay is never worried about going beyond the law. Indeed he deems the processes of law to be useless in the face of large-scale evil. He is a maverick, and he is a leader of men rather than someone who happily takes orders. He enjoys the responsibility which he achieves during the dénouement at the end of the book, though he likes to play down his own importance. He is modest, brusque, utterly honest and reliablc, forthright, fit and strong, and endowed with a sense of irony and sportsmanship. Buchan was sufficiently pleased with his creation of Richard Hannay to use him as the protagonist in four more novels after *The Thirty-Nine Steps.* In Hannay he deliberately constructed his own version of a famous type, an example of the English officer and gentleman. He added the ironical twist that his English gentleman was in fact a South African of poor origin.

There are naturally many points at which John Buchan the author and Richard Hannay his created narrator intersect. In his autobiography, *Memory Hold-the-Door* (1940), Buchan describes his admiration and love for the shepherds of the Border countryside where he grew up:

> Those Border shepherds, the men of the long stride and the clear eye, were a great race – I have never known a greater. The narrower kinds of fanaticism which have run riot elsewhere in Scotland, rarely affected the Borders. Their people were 'grave livers', in Wordsworth's phrase, God-fearing, decent in all the relations of life, and supreme masters of their craft. They were a fighting stock because of their ancestry, and of a noble independence. As the source of the greatest ballads in any literature they had fire and imagination, and some aptitude for the graces of life. They lacked the dourness of the conventional Scot, having a quick eye for comedy, and, being in themselves wholly secure, they were aristocrats with the fine manners of an aristocracy. By them I was admitted into the secrets of a whole lost world of pastoral. I acquired a reverence and affection for the 'plain people', who to Walter Scott and Abraham Lincoln were what mattered most in the world. (pp.23–4)

This sober and nostalgic analysis may differ in tone from Hannay's impulsive descriptions, but the creative impulse behind such characters as Alexander Turnbull or the other kind country folk who care for Hannay during his flight becomes clearer. Similarly something of Hannay's distrust or dislike of the middle classes emerges in Buchan's autobiography:

> As a child I was always in terror of being compelled to earn my bread as a clerk should my father die. This gloomy fate I associated with some kind of English domicile, probably a London suburb. The suburbs of the metropolis, of which I knew nothing, became for me a synonym for a dreadful life of commercial drudgery without daylight or hope. (p.46)

Like Hannay, Buchan admired sportsmanship, and was a passionate fisherman and a good shot. Like Hannay he knew southern Africa well. The points of comparison are many and clear, but this does not deny the force of the earlier statement, that it is necessary to remember when considering *The Thirty-Nine Steps* that Hannay is not Buchan: it is only through understanding Hannay as an invention, a created fiction, as a literary artifact rather than an offshoot of Buchan's life and personality, that Buchan's achievement can be understood.

The plot

The plot is partly devised to show Hannay travelling through picturesque scenery, and making contact with a broad spectrum of different types and classes of person. Buchan gives another reason in *Memory Hold-the-Door* for constructing his adventure stories in the mould of the journey or chase:

> I generally thought of a character or two, and then a set of incidents and the question was how my people would behave. They had the knack of just squeezing out of unpleasant places and of bringing their doings to a rousing climax.
>
> I was especially fascinated by the notion of hurried journeys. In the great romances of literature they provide some of the chief dramatic moments, and since the theme is common to Homer and the penny reciter it must appeal to a very ancient instinct in human nature. We live our lives under the twin categories of time and space, and when the two come into conflict we get the great moment. Whether failure or success is the result, life is sharpened, intensified, idealised. A long journey, even with the most lofty purpose, may be a dull thing to read of if it is made at leisure; but a hundred yards may be a breathless business if only a few seconds are granted to complete it. For then it becomes a sporting event, a race; and the interest which makes millions read of the Derby is the same, in a grosser form, as when we follow an expedition straining to relieve a beleaguered fort, or a man fleeing to a sanctuary with the avenger behind him. (pp.193–4)

Buchan's fascination with this theme in literature led him to publish a collection of such stories, *A Book of Escapes and Hurried Journeys* (1922). Most of his novels include journeys which have to be undertaken against specially difficult odds, and his first Hannay novel is no exception. In the first few pages of *The Thirty-Nine Steps* we are given the date of the Black Stone's intended assault on European political stability, and by the end of the second chapter Hannay is engaged in a 'hurried journey'. With speed and directness Buchan engages our interest in 'the twin categories of time and space'. At first suspense hangs on the chase in Scotland. After Hannay has met Sir Walter Bullivant, the action still depends on future events, first on what exactly the Black Stone will do, secondly on the problem of solving the mystery of the thirty-nine steps, and thirdly on the last minute successful capture of the German spies. At all points in the story when some part of the plot is resolved, there are developments which throw the reader's interest further into the book's future, thus always keeping the reader in expectation of more action.

The plot indeed moves so fast that the reader happily suspends his disbelief in the more sensational or unlikely aspects. Hannay chooses arbitrarily to hide in Scotland, and after zig-zagging on foot, by car and bicycle for several days, when he is within minutes of being caught by the police, he finds himself seeking sanctuary in the garden of a remote country house which, it transpires, just happens to be the headquarters of his arch-enemy. It is a coincidence of the most extreme kind, yet in the imaginary world of spies, disguise and hot pursuit that Hannay inhabits, it seems perfectly natural, and any misgivings or doubts are soon forgotten by the reader in the helter-skelter of developing events. Nevertheless, the later Hannay novels do not contain such perilous assaults on the reader's credibility.

The romance

Buchan knows well that some of the events of his story are unlikely in the extreme. At times he seems to enjoy playing with our credibility. Although his characterisation and description aim at verisimilitude, *The Thirty-Nine Steps* is not as a whole a realistic work, as the occasional overstretched coincidence suggests. In *Memory Hold-the-Door* Buchan loosely classifies all his fictional writing as 'romance'. He describes the Richard Hannay stories as 'forthright tales of adventure', contrasting them with his more serious historical fictions. He tells of their casual origin and how *The Thirty-Nine Steps* was conceived and written for his own amusement:

> Then, while pinned to my bed during the first months of war and compelled to keep my mind off too tragic realities, I gave myself to stories of adventure. I invented a young South African called Richard Hannay, who had traits copied from my friends, and I amused myself with considering what he would do in various emergencies. In *The Thirty-Nine Steps* he was spy-hunting in Britain; in *Greenmantle* he was on a mission to the East; and in *Mr Standfast*, published in 1919, he was busy in Scotland and France. The first had an immediate success, and, since that kind of thing seemed to amuse my friends in the trenches, I was encouraged to continue. (p.196)

He shows a similar dismissive modesty in his dedication of *The Thirty-*

Nine Steps to T. A. Nelson, his publishing friend.

> My dear Tommy
> You and I have long cherished an affection for that elementary type of tale which Americans call the 'dime novel' and which we know as the 'shocker'—the romance where the incidents defy the probabilities, and march just inside the borders of the possible. During an illness last winter I exhausted my store of those aids to cheerfulness, and was driven to write one for myself. This little volume is the result, and I should like to put your name on it in memory of our long friendship, in the days when the wildest fictions are so much less improbable than the facts.
>
> J.B.

Here Buchan shows the deliberation with which he has pushed the incidents of his story 'just inside the borders of the possible'. And again he defines his 'shocker' as a 'romance'.

Romance is perhaps an odd word with which to describe *The Thirty-Nine Steps*, and requires some explanation. In origin, in medieval literature, romances were fictional adventure stories, of chivalry or love, in verse or prose. They were works of entertainment, not particularly serious or didactic, and they usually depicted characters living in a world remote from everyday life, who performed deeds of superhuman courage and gallantry, often aided by fantastic or magical forces. The tradition is satirised in *Don Quixote de la Mancha* (Part 1 published in 1605, part 2 in 1612) by Miguel de Cervantes (1547–1616). *Don Quixote* is one of the earliest prose fictions in European literature to fulfil certain modern criteria for the novel, so it is often cited as the first novel. Ironically it is more famous than any of the romances which it satirises.

Several elements in *The Thirty-Nine Steps* show why Buchan calls it a romance. There are the strongly improbable coincidences and ironic reversals of the plot. Every time Hannay is on the brink of being caught by his opponents, some wonderfully lucky event occurs which prevents his capture—meeting the roadmender, or nearly driving his car into Sir Harry, or bumping into Marmaduke Jopley in the middle of Scotland. Admittedly these events are to an extent balanced by the equally spectacular misfortune of seeking refuge in the enemy headquarters, but even his escape from there, aided by explosives left in an adjoining cupboard, defies probability.

Hannay himself is not aided by magic or superhuman qualities, though he is a very fit thirty-seven-year-old. Still, he has little to do with the ordinary world of everyday existence: his listlessness and boredom at the beginning of the book show this. He is someone to whom remote and extraordinary events attach themselves: he is scarcely surprised when Scudder rushes into his apartment with an amazing story of international espionage. Equally Hannay happily shoulders the burden of diverting the First World War completely on his own.

One ingredient common to most romances which is not to be found in *The Thirty-Nine Steps* is love. Buchan remedies this in *Mr Standfast* (1919) where Hannay falls in love with Mary Lamington, whom he marries, and who is to assist him in all his latter adventures. The several film adaptations of *The Thirty-Nine Steps* have also overcome this omission simply by adding quantities of exotic female spies to Buchan's original plot.

By calling his novels romances in contrast with his historical and biographical writings Buchan draws attention to the fact that they are primarily intended as harmless entertainment; he likes to play down any serious purpose in these works. As a student he had attempted a more pretentious kind of writing, and as he says in *Memory Hold-the-Door* (p.194) 'had then some ambition to write fiction in the grand manner, by interpreting and clarifying a large piece of life,' but this ambition waned. Inventing Hannay was pure relaxation:

> It was huge fun playing with my puppets, and to me they soon became very real flesh and blood. I never consciously invented with a pen in my hand; I waited until the story had told itself and then wrote it down, and, since it was already a finished thing, I wrote it fast. The books had a wide sale, both in English and in translations, and I always felt a little ashamed that profit should accrue from what had given me so much amusement. I had no purpose in such writing except to please myself, and even if my books had not found a single reader I would have felt amply repaid. (pp.195–6)

Buchan and Sir Walter Scott

In characterising himself so casually as a 'story-teller' and as a writer of romances, Buchan may have been imitating the similarly casual and unpretentious literary stance of the greatest Scottish novelist, Sir Walter Scott. Many characteristic features of the Hannay books, including *The Thirty-Nine Steps*, are more or less conscious imitations or allusions to the methods and interests of Scott's famous *Waverley* novels, with the important distinctions that Buchan writes about contemporary rather than historical events, and that Buchan aims his book at a wider popular audience.

Scott, like Buchan, favoured the journey or escape as a simple but useful plot-framework. Likewise his novels abound with descriptions of landscape, particularly the Scottish Highlands. Scott was probably the first novelist to feature natural description and the picturesque as a coherent element in the novel form, as has since become common amongst nearly all novelists. In some parts of Scott's novels the depiction of the characters in their surroundings has a symbolic value beyond its intrinsic interest.

A journey plot makes this description of changing scenery natural and almost inevitable. In just the same way the hero of a novel on a journey can be made to meet a succession of different people in unusual circumstances whose variety and eccentricity will spice the narrative. Scott and Buchan, then, share a delight in creating vivid and multifarious minor characters in their novels, characters who cut across distinctions of class and nationality.

Scott's first novel, *Waverley* (1814), contains all these elements which recur in Buchan's writing. The young hero loses himself in the Scottish Highlands, is pursued for different reasons by forces who are at odds with each other, is hidden when ill, finds himself caught up in violent action, and so on. The main themes of *Waverley*—the relationships of patriotism and loyalty with ideological fanaticism, and escapism with hard practical reality, and the nature of action—are also comparable with Buchan's main concerns as they are manifested during his whole literary career, though Buchan is less equivocal than Scott in his admiration for single minded and strongly active patriotism.

Other Scottish writers, notably Robert Louis Stevenson (1850–94) in *Kidnapped* (1886) and its sequel *Catriona* (1893), have reworked the adventurous journey in a manner reminiscent of Scott, and this strand of romantic picaresque amounts to an identifiable tradition in Scottish literature. In his youth Buchan admired Stevenson, but Scott was the writer whom he revered constantly and highly throughout his lifetime. He went so far as to describe his biography, *Sir Walter Scott*, as a 'literary *credo*' and a 'confession of faith' (*Memory Hold-the-Door* p.199).

To sum up, *The Thirty-Nine Steps* is a combination of many varied literary styles and influences. Primarily it is a 'shocker', an entertainment aimed at a large popular audience, like the novels of E. Phillips Oppenheim (1866–1946), now little read but much enjoyed by Buchan and his contemporaries. It is also written in a tradition of Scottish adventure stories like those of Robert Louis Stevenson. And in some of its interests and methods it is reminiscent of the originator of these Scottish romances, Sir Walter Scott. It is also, of course, a spy story and its focus on espionage is a new element brought into the traditional romance framework by Buchan.

The spy story

The time of publication of *The Thirty-Nine Steps* gave it a purpose somewhat more serious than purely frivolous entertainment. The First World War began in the summer of 1914 and *The Thirty-Nine Steps* was first published in serial form in *Blackwood's Magazine* during the summer of the following year. It was written to amuse Buchan's 'friends in the trenches', and in its romance-like world of clear-cut good and evil it is a work of propaganda, intended to bolster the morale of those who read it. The literature of spying provides a very useful barometer to the changing degree of patriotism and cynicism during the twentieth century.

Stories about espionage nowadays form an identifiable sub-group within the broad spectrum of the novel genre. They are a relatively recent development, starting in the late nineteenth century, an early exponent of the form being the now little-read journalist and writer of thrillers William Le Queux (1864–1927), who may possibly have been a spy himself and who wrote about thirty novels about spying. Several other spy stories were written before the First World War, including *Kim* (1901) by Rudyard Kipling (1865–1936), *The Riddle of the Sands* (1903) by Erskine Childers (1870–1922), *The Secret Agent* (1907) and *Under Western Eyes* (1911) by Joseph Conrad (1857–1924). The war gave rise to an atmosphere of patriotic righteousness in which spy stories with a simple nationalistic, anti-German message, like *The Thirty-Nine Steps*, would thrive. At the same time as writing the Richard Hannay adventures, from late 1914 onwards, Buchan was involved in writing his popular history of the war in monthly volumes, which received special government approval and was in effect part of the British propaganda machine. Later Buchan was invited to found what became the Ministry of Information, the source and control of British propaganda. He was a patriot but by no means a warmonger, and though his adventure stories are patently and straightforwardly pro-British, he never descends to the simple-minded chauvinism which often characterises the popular literature of wartime. Indeed in his second Hannay novel, *Greenmantle*, his protagonist actually meets the Kaiser on a railway platform, and Britain's enemy is described, relatively sympathetically, as a tired old man.

But the Hannay stories still present a heroic or even romantic view of espionage. *The Thirty-Nine Steps* shows a battle between good and evil, in which courage prevails against mendacious cunning. Later spy stories, starting with those of Somerset Maugham (1874–1965) in *Ashenden* (1928), show spies as ordinary people, involved in a mundane, even sordid job. They are realistic thrillers rather than romances. During the nineteen-thirties and forties Eric Ambler (b.1909) and Grahame Greene (b.1904) wrote painstakingly credible and unglamorous tales of espionage, but the trend towards realism in the form was reversed first by the Second World War, with a return to crude nationalism, and secondly by the success of books by Ian Fleming. (1908–64). His creation, James Bond is a secret service protagonist of absurdly slick, almost superhuman qualities of the kind that make Hannay look thoroughly dowdy by contrast. Bond's enemies are diabolically evil madmen intent on mastering the world with the help of the Russian secret service. These exaggerated tales have been made into glamorous and successful films famous for their violence and mild eroticism.

The nineteen-sixties saw a complete reaction to the glossy and fantastic struggles of Bond. Novels by Len Deighton (b.1929) and John LeCarré (b.1931), respectively *The Ipcress File* (1963) and *The Spy Who Came In From The Cold* (1963), depict spies in an even more anti-heroic mode than those of Maugham, Ambler and Greene: they concentrate on the ruthless deliberation, cruelty and cynicism of the spying machinery of opposed powers during the Cold War.

A very large number of spy stories by the writers mentioned above have been best sellers and have made their authors huge sums of money. Clearly espionage as a subject for fiction has a special fascination even during peacetime. Buchan's novels too have kept their popular appeal and have been reprinted many times during the last seventy years.

Disguise

The success of the anti-heroic spy story suggests that it is not merely the simplification of the world into friend and enemy, good and evil, which captures the popular imagination. One factor common to all spy stories by their very nature is disguise. Spies must disguise their real motives, feelings and beliefs in order to exist in an alien society. Hannay's enemies are masters of disguise in *The Thirty-Nine Steps* and he too has to adopt different roles—a milkman, a Scots farmer, a roadmender, an Australian politician, a vagrant and a shepherd, to mention but a few—in order to match and defeat their evil. All the Hannay novels describe extraordinary (and unrealistic) feats of impersonation, and in *The Thirty-Nine Steps* there is something of a debate about the nature of adopting roles and of deceiving one's enemies. There is the elaborate description of Hannay's impersonation of the roadmender, almost a guide for aspiring actors, with its emphasis on 'living the part'. Secondly there is the discussion that follows the impersonation of Lord Alloa by the Black Stone spy, including the tale of the camouflaged lion told by General Roger. Thirdly there are Hannay's reflections about the Black Stone's disguise before his final arrest of the spy ring:

> Peter once discussed with me the question of disguises, and he had a theory which struck me at the time. He said, barring absolute certainties like fingerprints, mere physical traits were very little use for identification if the fugitive really knew his business. He laughed at things like dyed hair and false beards and such childish follies. The only thing that mattered was what Peter called 'atmosphere'.
>
> If a man could get into perfectly different surroundings from those in which he had been first observed, and—this is the important part—really play up to these surroundings and behave as if he had never been out of them, he would puzzle the cleverest detectives on earth. And he used to tell a story of how he once borrowed a black coat and went to church and shared the same hymn-book with the man that was looking for him. If that man had seen him in decent company before he would have recognised him; but he had only seen him snuffing the lights in a public-house with a revolver.

Peter Pienaar is to figure more in the later Hannay novels. Buchan is obviously fascinated by disguise, or at least wants to intrigue his readers by this 'realistic' discussion: the false beards and other props beloved by, say, Sherlock Holmes, are dispensed with.

Buchan's interest in disguise may be interpreted in three ways all of which are interconnected. Firstly, as readers we virtually adopt the disguise of Hannay: our imaginative identification with his adventure, transporting us, as we sit quietly reading, into a world of vigorous action, violence, and the excitement of the chase, is comparable with Hannay's ability to imagine himself as the roadmender. Secondly, the analysis of disguise reminds us of the way in which we can be deceived into not seeing what struggles of good and evil, what excitement, and what strangeness may lie just below the surface of the familiar world. Thirdly, the spy, whose internal and external existences are so much at odds with each other, and whose whole life must be an elaborate deception, is almost an allegory of modern man, so often condemned to a dull, urban routine, trapped as he is in a way of life which will not easily allow the expression of his imaginative or idealised longings. We all sense at some time this disparity between our own view of ourselves as full of latent potential, and our knowledge of how others see us diminished and fixed in character. The imagined world of romance, though it may be escapist and illusory, is about just this conflict between the ordinary and the idealised, and disguise is the metaphor for our escape from a dreary and monotonous reality, the escape which Buchan provides and describes in his tales of adventure.

Part 4

Hints for study

Use of summaries

Part 2 of these Notes consists of summaries of the main events and action of the book. Never treat these summaries as if they give anything more than a skeletal outline of the story. It is in the difference between the summaries and the book itself that Buchan's skill as a writer can best be observed. The summaries trivialise the plot, reducing the book to its most meagre dimension. Buchan's style, his characterisation, both of Hannay and of the people Hannay meets, and his descriptive powers are all completely lost in the summarisation of the action.

Nevertheless you should try to write your own summaries of the book. Reread a chapter carefully and then describe what happens in your own words. Compare your summary with the summary in this book, to see if you agree about the chief details.

Plot

It is necessary to have a good grasp of the plot of the story. Buchan's ten chapter headings are clear signposts to the main events of the novel. These titles and their proper order should be memorised as a convenient way of grasping the book's overall action. *The Thirty-Nine Steps* is not a complicated book and its plot is simple and straightforward, though it is easily possible to muddle the events of Hannay's escape and flight as the order of 'adventures' is somewhat arbitrary.

Style

A writer's style can be discerned in his choice of vocabulary and grammatical constructions. It is an elusive quality which can be difficult to define. Some awareness of literary style is best achieved through a student's consciousness of his own stylistic traits. Every sentence, spoken or written, whether by a writer, a critic or a student, is the consequence of a series of choices about individual words and about the best order for those words. A student who is aware of this process of choice has the capacity to understand why Buchan should have chosen the individual words, phrases and metaphors that occur in any particular passage in *The Thirty-Nine Steps*. Thus the best training in learning to appreciate literary style is the attempt to write for oneself.

Try describing a piece of landscape with the same kind of clarity and flair that Buchan uses in his writing. Imagine that you, like Hannay, are being chased, so that a speedy analysis of the surroundings is vital to your safety. Or imagine what one of the policemen chasing Hannay might have felt or seen as the chase develops speed in Chapter 5. Do not write a scientific description, and do not mention every detail at tedious length. Try, like Buchan, to find a metaphor or comparison or a way of describing the landscape that creates a vivid image in the mind of your reader. Reread the relevant passages in Chapter 5 and the discussion of Buchan's style in the Commentary (in Part 3 of these notes) so as to recognise for yourself the way in which Buchan goes about describing landscape.

Characterisation

Try to describe an encounter with a slightly unusual person, such as the spectacled roadman. Choose the details of dress and behaviour that characterise his uniqueness. Include some kind of conversation, and give his speech a special quality that separates what he says quite clearly from the surrounding description and adds to your reader's appreciation of the character.

Reread some of Buchan's descriptions of people so as to identify the kind of detail he likes to choose in order to bring his creations to life, particularise them and make them unique.

Hannay

Make a list of what you consider to be the episodes or comments which most clearly illustrate Richard Hannay's character as invented by Buchan. Are there any parts of the book where you disapprove of Hannay's behaviour or attitude? If there are, can you explain exactly why you disapprove?

Credibility

What parts of the plot seem to you to be least believable, least likely to have happened? Is the book spoilt by its incredible episodes, if there are any?

Specimen questions

(1) Describe the main features of Richard Hannay's character in *The Thirty-Nine Steps.*

(2) Why does Buchan tell the story of *The Thirty-Nine Steps* from Hannay's point of view?

(3) Choose any two minor characters from *The Thirty-Nine Steps*, examine Buchan's technique in creating them, and show what they add to the plot and the atmosphere of the book.

(4) Write an imitation 'adventure' of Richard Hannay, describing events from his point of view, and attempting to copy the way in which Buchan creates Hannay's character from inside, through his language and the way in which he views events.

(5) How does Buchan maintain the suspense in *The Thirty-Nine Steps*?

(6) Does Buchan make Hannay's adventures too improbable in *The Thirty-Nine Steps*?

(7) What are Buchan's best and worst qualities as a writer in *The Thirty-Nine Steps*?

(8) Does *The Thirty-Nine Steps* seem to you to have any serious artistic purpose or is it, as Buchan called it, just a 'shocker'.

A specimen answer

Choose any two minor characters from *The Thirty-Nine Steps*, examine Buchan's technique in creating them, and show what they add to the plot and atmosphere of the book.

Franklin P. Scudder, 'The Man Who Died' in Chapter 1 of *The Thirty-Nine Steps*, and Sir Harry, 'The Radical Candidate' of Chapter 4, are markedly different kinds of people invented by Buchan as foils for his central character, the narrator Richard Hannay. Both of them also advance Buchan's plot: Scudder initiates the whole adventure of *The Thirty-Nine Steps*, while Sir Harry's car crash diversifies the chase which occupies most of the first two-thirds of the book.

The way Scudder bursts into Hannay's flat and the extraordinary story of international espionage which he babbles to Hannay are typical of the 'shocker', Buchan's term for this kind of novel. Hannay at first thinks him mad or drunk. The contrast between Scudder's excitement and Hannay, who stays cool and calm, is clear.

Scudder introduces himself to Hannay with the melodramatic announcement that he is himself dead. It is not until we learn how he has tried to escape his pursuers by disguising a corpse as himself that we understand this bizarre comment. Buchan likes to catch his readers' attention with a mystery, the resolution of which is delayed for as long as possible. Scudder's explanation of his 'death' is a minor illustration of this technique.

Scudder is also responsible for one of the major mysteries of the novel. His notebook contains the coded information which Hannay has to unravel in order to learn more about his enemies, but it is not until Chapter 9 that the meaning of the 'thirty-nine steps' becomes known.

Scudder's speech is dominated by Americanisms. He starts several sentences with the exhortation 'Say' and his vocabulary is peppered with American expressions, such as 'I reckon' and 'it's a mighty liberty'. This contrasts with Hannay's language, which Buchan makes colloquial, especially in the opening pages, but which is British and colonial in its vocabulary. Buchan's capacity to imitate different accents is displayed throughout the book, but nowhere better than in this opening encounter between Scudder and Hannay.

Scudder's flight across Europe pursued by murderous spies and the discovery of his body with a knife stuck in its back typify the unusual and adventurous world of *The Thirty-Nine Steps*. In his story he provides a miniature version of the plot of the whole book, and a suggestive introduction to its atmosphere of violence and danger. He also initiates one of the book's underlying themes, and one which seems to have specially fascinated Buchan. Scudder is 'no slouch at disguises', and in this reincarnation as a Gurkha officer, Captain Digby, he provides the first example of the many different disguises which occur throughout the book (though we have already heard of his skills in this direction in his attempts to escape the Black Stone).

When Hannay meets Sir Walter Bullivant we learn more about Scudder's character. Sir Walter distrusts him as a secret agent because of his independence and his hot-headed prejudices, notably his anti-Semitism. But when they hear of the assassination of Karolides, Scudder's judgement appears to have been proved accurate. Scudder's anti-Semitic ideas, which he expresses to Hannay in Chapter 1, have been taken by some critics to represent Buchan's own prejudices in this direction, though it would be wrong to assume that an author shares or even condones the attitudes and points of view of his invented characters.

Sir Harry advances the plot of *The Thirty-Nine Steps* by arranging the encounter between Hannay and Sir Walter Bullivant. Even this contributes to the book's suspense, as the rendezvous is planned long before it happens. Apart from providing this necessary link, which ultimately allows Hannay to scotch the Black Stone's plans, Sir Harry is a relatively minor figure in the novel, though he acts as another convenient foil for Hannay and provokes an entertaining episode in the Scottish chase.

Hannay usually comes upon the people he meets suddenly, and his encounter with Sir Harry is no exception: Hannay is forced to crash his car into a ravine. This incident is typical of the sudden reversals in the book, though the car accident turns out to be a stroke of good fortune for Hannay since it diverts the spy gang from his trail, as well as allowing him time for a much needed meal and a new suit of clothes.

We first see Sir Harry 'whinnying apologies' for his bad driving, dressed in the incongruous garb of the early motorist. Buchan usually introduces his characters in this way, choosing for them some typifying mode of behaviour which suggests their unique identity and helps to create an atmosphere of reality. Scudder's first action after bursting into Hannay's flat is to rush around, searching the rooms and locking the doors, before helping himself to a whisky, and these curious actions are similar inventions for the purpose of establishing and defining his character.

Sir Harry is characterised as an innocent and pleasant but slightly foolish young man, in contrast to the experienced and tough Hannay. Sir Harry expects Hannay to speak at an electoral meeting about Australian politics, even though he has just nearly killed him in a car accident: this suggests his impulsive, disorganised and thoughtless nature. Sir Harry's speech is 'the most appalling rot', and the conservative Buchan contrasts Hannay's world of direct action with these liberal policies, which the Black Stone's plot and the melodramatic events of *The Thirty-Nine Steps* prove to be utterly mistaken. Yet Buchan makes Sir Harry likeable for his generosity and awkward honesty. Hannay enjoys Sir Harry's enthusiasm for horse-racing and shooting, regarding knowledge of these pastimes as a truer guide to character than nonsensical political jargon.

The adventure of 'The Radical Candidate' is a short interlude for Hannay in the middle of his desparate flight on the moors, a parenthetic excursion into the world of country houses and well-connected young aristocrats. The genteel ease of Sir Harry's 'big, cheery smoking-room, with a crackling wood fire' is a complete contrast to the world of the other simple country folk, like the roadmender, who help Hannay. This kind of contrast adds to the book's variety and richness. Hannay's values, and perhaps ultimately Buchan's, can be detected in the good qualities of the people who help him.

Buchan takes care to weave his minor characters into the plot. He describes them by means of carefully chosen significant details, almost exaggerating certain aspects of their behaviour. Sir Harry is almost a caricature of the callow young gentleman, while Scudder, with his extraordinary tale of anarchists and murder, his vivid American accent and his bizarre death, plunges the reader into the melodramatic world of espionage and provides a gripping and mysterious opening to *The*

Thirty-Nine Steps. One of the chief attractions of Buchan's stories is his talent for creating minor characters. Scudder and Sir Harry are contrasting but equally excellent examples of Buchan's skill in this direction.

Some points for discussion

(1) Does the essay deal adequately with both Scudder and Sir Harry?

(2) Does the writer of the specimen answer say enough about the atmosphere of *The Thirty-Nine Steps*?

(3) Can you think of any useful details or facts about the two characters which are not mentioned in the essay?

(4) Are Scudder and Sir Harry a good choice out of the various minor characters in the book for the purpose of answering this question?

(5) Is any of the material mentioned in the essay not strictly relevant to the question asked? What could be cut out?

Part 5

Suggestions for further reading

The text

The text of *The Thirty-Nine Steps* used in these notes is that published by Pan Books, London and Sydney, 1947; 30th printing, 1976.

Other novels by Buchan

The following is a list of John Buchan's novels with their dates of publication. This is more of a guide to Buchan's career than a bibliographical tool. It does not include his books of history, biography, poetry, his collections of short stories, or his innumerable journalistic essays.

Sir Quixote of the Moors (1895)
John Burnet of Barns (1898)
A Lost Lady of Old Years (1899)
The Half-Hearted (1900)
Prester John (1910)
The Thirty-Nine Steps (1915)
The Power-House (1916)
Greenmantle (1916)
Mr Standfast (1918)
The Path of the King (1921)
Huntingtower (1922)
Midwinter (1923)
The Three Hostages (1924)
John Macnab (1925)
The Dancing Floor (1926)
Witch Wood (1927)
The Courts of the Morning (1929)
Castle Gay (1930)
The Blanket of the Dark (1931)
The Gap in the Curtain (1932)
A Prince of the Captivity (1933)
The Free Fishers (1934)
The House of the Four Winds (1935)
The Island of Sheep (1936)
The Interpreter's House (1938)
Sick Heart River (1941)

The five Richard Hannay novels are *The Thirty-Nine Steps*, *Greenmantle*, *Mr Standfast*, *The Three Hostages*, and *The Island of Sheep*. Hannay also appears in *The Courts of the Morning*.

Buchan created two other characters who act as the protagonists for more than one book. Sir Edward Leithen, a London lawyer, is the hero of *The Power House*, *John Macnab*, *The Dancing Floor*, *The Gap in the Curtain* and *Sick Heart River*. Dickson McCunn, a retired grocer from Glasgow, in deliberate contrast to Hannay and Leithen, is the hero in *Huntingtower*, *Castle Gay*, and *The House of the Four Winds*.

Buchan's life

Buchan's autobiography, *Memory Hold-the-Door*, Hodder and Stoughton, London, 1946, provides a fascinating inward view of his opinions and career. The best biography, *John Buchan*, is by Janet Adam Smith, Hart-Davis, London, 1965.

Critical works

The following are general critical studies, not devoted solely to *The Thirty-Nine Steps*.

DANIELL, DAVID: *The Interpreter's House*, Nelson, London, 1975.

HIMMELFARB, GERTRUDE: 'John Buchan: the Last Victorian,' in *Victorian Minds*, Weidenfeld and Nicholson, London, 1968: strongly critical of Buchan's views and achievement.

SANDISON, A.: 'John Buchan: the Church of Empire' in *Wheel of Empire*, Macmillan, London, 1967.

USBORNE, RICHARD: *Clubland Heroes: A Nostalgic Study of Some Recurrent Characters in the Romantic Fiction of Dornford Yates, Buchan and Sapper*, Constable, London, 1953. A pleasantly mocking study.

Bibliography

A useful, relatively recent list of books by and about Buchan is to be found in Volume 4 of *The New Cambridge Bibliography of English Literature*, Cambridge University Press, Cambridge, 1972.

The author of these notes

MARTIN GRAY was educated at the Universities of Perugia, Oxford and London. After two years teaching English at the University of Leicester he became a lecturer in the Department of English Studies at Stirling. He is joint author of *The Penguin Book of The Bicycle* (1978) and is compiling the *York Dictionary of Literary Terms* which is to accompany the York Notes series.

YORK NOTES

The first 100 titles

CHINUA ACHEBE	*Arrow of God* *Things Fall Apart*
JANE AUSTEN	*Northanger Abbey* *Pride and Prejudice* *Sense and Sensibility*
ROBERT BOLT	*A Man For All Seasons*
CHARLOTTE BRONTË	*Jane Eyre*
EMILY BRONTË	*Wuthering Heights*
ALBERT CAMUS	*L'Etranger (The Outsider)*
GEOFFREY CHAUCER	*Prologue to the Canterbury Tales* *The Franklin's Tale* *The Knight's Tale* *The Nun's Priest's Tale* *The Pardoner's Tale*
SIR ARTHUR CONAN DOYLE	*The Hound of the Baskervilles*
JOSEPH CONRAD	*Nostromo*
DANIEL DEFOE	*Robinson Crusoe*
CHARLES DICKENS	*David Copperfield* *Great Expectations*
GEORGE ELIOT	*Adam Bede* *Silas Marner* *The Mill on the Floss*
T.S. ELIOT	*The Waste Land*
WILLIAM FAULKNER	*As I Lay Dying*
F. SCOTT FITZGERALD	*The Great Gatsby*
E.M. FORSTER	*A Passage to India*
ATHOL FUGARD	*Selected Plays*

MRS GASKELL	*North and South*
WILLIAM GOLDING	*Lord of the Flies*
OLIVER GOLDSMITH	*The Vicar of Wakefield*
THOMAS HARDY	*Jude the Obscure* *Tess of the D'Urbervilles* *The Mayor of Casterbridge* *The Return of the Native* *The Trumpet Major*
L.P. HARTLEY	*The Go-Between*
ERNEST HEMINGWAY	*For Whom the Bell Tolls* *The Old Man and the Sea*
ANTHONY HOPE	*The Prisoner of Zenda*
RICHARD HUGHES	*A High Wind in Jamaica*
THOMAS HUGHES	*Tom Brown's Schooldays*
HENRIK IBSEN	*A Doll's House*
HENRY JAMES	*The Turn of the Screw*
BEN JONSON	*The Alchemist* *Volpone*
D.H. LAWRENCE	*Sons and Lovers* *The Rainbow*
HARPER LEE	*To Kill a Mocking-Bird*
SOMERSET MAUGHAM	*Selected Short Stories*
HERMAN MELVILLE	*Billy Budd* *Moby Dick*
ARTHUR MILLER	*Death of a Salesman* *The Crucible*
JOHN MILTON	*Paradise Lost I & II*
SEAN O'CASEY	*Juno and the Paycock*
GEORGE ORWELL	*Animal Farm* *Nineteen Eighty-four*
JOHN OSBORNE	*Look Back in Anger*
HAROLD PINTER	*The Birthday Party*
J.D. SALINGER	*The Catcher in the Rye*

SIR WALTER SCOTT	*Ivanhoe* *Quentin Durward*
WILLIAM SHAKESPEARE	*A Midsummer Night's Dream* *Antony and Cleopatra* *Coriolanus* *Cymbeline* *Hamlet* *Henry IV Part I* *Henry V* *Julius Caesar* *King Lear* *Macbeth* *Measure for Measure* *Othello* *Richard II* *Romeo and Juliet* *The Merchant of Venice* *The Tempest* *The Winter's Tale* *Troilus and Cressida* *Twelfth Night*
GEORGE BERNARD SHAW	*Androcles and the Lion* *Arms and the Man* *Caesar and Cleopatra* *Pygmalion*
RICHARD BRINSLEY SHERIDAN	*The School for Scandal*
JOHN STEINBECK	*Of Mice and Men* *The Grapes of Wrath* *The Pearl*
ROBERT LOUIS STEVENSON	*Kidnapped* *Treasure Island*
JONATHAN SWIFT	*Gulliver's Travels*
W.M. THACKERAY	*Vanity Fair*
MARK TWAIN	*Huckleberry Finn* *Tom Sawyer*
VOLTAIRE	*Candide*
H.G. WELLS	*The History of Mr Polly* *The Invisible Man* *The War of the Worlds*
OSCAR WILDE	*The Importance of Being Earnest*